T0246033

YOU SHALL BE AS GODS

Pagans, Progressives, and the
Rise of the Woke Gnostic Left

ERICK ERICKSON

BOMBARDIER
BOOKS

Published by Bombardier Books
An Imprint of Post Hill Press
ISBN: 979-8-88845-068-0
ISBN (eBook): 979-8-88845-069-7

You Shall Be as Gods:
Pagans, Progressives, and the Rise of the Woke Gnostic Left
© 2024 by Erick Erickson
All Rights Reserved

Cover Design by Jim Villaflores

Post Hill Press
New York • Nashville
posthillpress.com

Published in the United States of America
1 2 3 4 5 6 7 8 9 10

TABLE OF CONTENTS

Chapter 1: A Crisis of Faith 1

Chapter 2: The New Ancient Religion 11

Chapter 3: The Judeo-Christian Vacuum:
            Accommodation and Compromise..................... 33

Chapter 4: Cultures in Conflict 67

Chapter 5: The Coming Violent Storm 94

Chapter 6: The Virus Spreads 118

Chapter 7: Be Angry, But Do Not Sin 140

Chapter 8: Love Your Neighbor 163

Chapter 9: Reconnect with Your Faith............................. 182

Chapter 10: Seek the Welfare of Your Community 204

Chapter 11: Let Go of Worry and Anxiety 224

Acknowledgments 249

CHAPTER 1

A CRISIS OF FAITH

*God is dead. God remains dead. And we have killed
him. How shall we comfort ourselves, the murderers
of all murderers? What was holiest and mighti-
est of all that the world has yet owned has bled to
death under our knives: who will wipe this blood
off us? What water is there for us to clean ourselves? What festivals of atonement, what sacred
games shall we have to invent? Is not the greatness
of this deed too great for us? Must we ourselves
not become gods simply to appear worthy of it?*
—Friedrich Nietzsche

n 2021, Pew Research released the results of a survey that
showed that nearly 30 percent of Americans consider themselves

unaffiliated with any religion.[1] The percentage of "Nones" doubled in just over a decade. In the same time period, self-identified Christians dropped from 75 percent to 63 percent of the population. Why are so many formerly professing Christians joining the ranks of the Nones? The numbers are stunning, and several people have tried to understand and explain the significance of this shift in religious affiliation.[2]

A common answer is politics. Sadly, politics has become all-consuming for many, including Christians. As one researcher explains, with the growing divide between the political sides in the United States, many of the Nones are struggling to find a place to belong: "They don't put up political yard signs. They don't go to political meetings. They feel left out, left behind, lost, unmoored, and disconnected from the larger society. They feel like society doesn't work for them."[3]

Churches, which should be a refuge from the world, have become increasingly partisan. Political beliefs and debates are fracturing relationships, families, and congregations. In response, a growing number of people are choosing to opt out of church altogether. But religion doesn't just go away. There are no real

[1] Gregory A. Smith, "About Three-in-Ten U.S. Adults Are Now Religiously Unaffiliated," Pew Research Center, December 14, 2021, https://www.pewresearch.org/religion/2021/12/14/about-three-in-ten-u-s-adults-are-now-religiously-unaffiliated/.

[2] See Mark L. Movsesian, "The Rise of the Nones," *Law & Liberty*, March 15, 2023, https://lawliberty.org/book-review/the-rise-of-the-nones/.

[3] Ryan Burge and Ann A. Michel, "Who are The Nones?: An In-Depth Interview with Ryan Burge," Lewis Center for Church Leadership, June 13, 2023, https://www.churchleadership.com/leading-ideas/who-are-the-nones-an-in-depth-interview-with-ryan-burge/.

atheists. Everyone places faith in something, worships something or someone, even if it's a humanist religion that worships the self.

Blaise Pascal is remembered for speaking of the God-shaped hole in everyone's heart. Paul explains in Romans 1 that humanity knows there is a God and that we should worship Him:

> For his invisible attributes, namely, his eternal power and divine nature, have been clearly perceived, ever since the creation of the world, in the things that have been made. So they are without excuse. For although they knew God, they did not honor him as God or give thanks to him, but they became futile in their thinking, and their foolish hearts were darkened. Claiming to be wise, they became fools. (Romans 1:20–22 ESV)

Left to our own devices, we will try to fill the God-shaped void in our lives with anything and everything imaginable. And that's what is happening even now when so many people claim to have no religion.

Defining Religion and Faith

How would you define religion? The dictionary definition seems straightforward at first glance: "a personal set or institutionalized system of religious attitudes, beliefs, and practices."[4] For Christianity, the set of attitudes, beliefs, and practices comes from the Bible and the traditions of the various denominations. The

---

4   *Merriam-Webster*, "Religion," https://www.merriam-webster.com/dictionary/religion.

basic beliefs include one triune God who created all things, who sent His Son to die on the cross for the sins of His people, and who hears prayers and answers them. Worship includes singing, praying, reading the Bible, listening to sermons, and participating in the sacraments. The number of sacraments—and how to practice them—varies, but the two that all denominations accept are baptism and communion. Believers profess faith in Christ for salvation. Christians look to their faith to guide how they live and treat others.

Every religion has beliefs that address questions like: How did the world and people come to exist? What does worship mean? What is the purpose of life? How should people treat others? Which behaviors should people engage in and which not? What happens after death? Even atheism and agnosticism offer answers of a sort to these questions.

An atheist might say the world and humanity evolved through scientific processes. The purpose of life is to live life to the fullest because there's nothing after death. While atheists might say they can't tell others how to live, they generally believe certain behaviors are right and others are wrong. They love their friends and family and believe they are basically good people. As far as worship, they may think they don't worship anyone or anything, but something in their life is of such ultimate importance to them that they would sacrifice much for it. It could be money, love or sex, a cause or purpose, or even the pursuit of happiness.

"What's in a name?" William Shakespeare once wrote. "A rose by any other name would smell as sweet." Meaning, call it a rose, or not a rose, it is still a rose. Call a rose an onion, and it will still smell nice. Even when we label a system of beliefs as atheism, religion is still religion. Although it may claim to be simply about there being no God, it remains a belief system about the nature and origin of life, the universe, and everything. It's important to remember that because, as we'll discuss, religious beliefs and faith play a central role in our lives and in our society.

Over the past fifty years, American society has tried—with some success—to push God, faith, and Christianity from public life, schools, businesses, and politics. But that doesn't mean religion is gone. In fact, a new religion is on the rise. What do I mean by a new religion? Well, going back to the dictionary definition, an alternative definition of religion is "a cause, principle, or system of beliefs held to with ardor and faith."[5] In the U.S. today, there is growing pressure to accept a certain system of beliefs. And as we're seeing, this new religion that doesn't call itself a religion does not want to co-exist peacefully with conservative, Judeo-Christian beliefs.

What in the World Is Happening?

That's the question being asked by so many Americans today. Many people feel as if reality itself has been turned upside down. Judeo-Christian values once taken for granted are not only routinely ignored, but openly attacked. And many people simply don't know how to respond. They don't agree with what's going on around them, but they care about their neighbors and they don't want to appear mean or unkind. So, they keep their heads down and go about life with their families, hoping that the mob

---

[5] Ibid.

won't come for them, but not sure what to do other than to rant and rave on social media. Maybe you're one of them.

Even those who are angry and fed up with it all aren't sure how to respond. Sure, it may feel good to rant, and voting for someone who "fights for us" may provide some small satisfaction in the moment—sort of a "take that" mentality—but at the end of the day, nothing changes.

Surely there must be a better way, a path to both understanding and responding to these attacks to shape deeper cultural change. There is, but it requires dealing with tough topics and being willing to understand how we got here in the first place and what we are truly up against at the root level, beneath all the clickbait headlines, fear, and angst.

The reason for all the crazy we see today is the influence of a religion that claims not to be a religion. In fact, it claims to be the anti-religion—when nothing could be further from the truth.

Back in 2016, I wrote *You Will Be Made to Care* in which I likened the Left's radical cultural agenda to a wildfire raging across our nation. What I said then was that it was just beginning to burn and that it would get worse before it burned itself out. The only question was how much cultural damage would be left behind. Unfortunately, we are seeing that fire burn today and popping up in many places.

I want to call out something in particular: The problem is not just on one side of the political spectrum. Yes, I do believe that the Democratic Party of today has been largely co-opted by those who seek to advance this radical, religious agenda. And it would be easy to dismiss it all as a partisan problem, thinking that if we all just vote Republican then the chaos will end. Not only does that approach come with its own problems, which I explore later in this book, but that partisan approach also misses the roots of the problem.

The bottom line is this: Our country doesn't have a partisan problem, a political problem, a social problem, or an economic problem. We have a spiritual problem. In the absence of God, Americans across partisan lines have turned to government and celebrity for their gods. They have gone off to worship idols. At the core, they have reverted to the original mistake made in the Garden of Eden: They choose to see themselves as gods.

The problem with viewing everything through a partisan lens is that neither side really wants to deal with the spiritual problem of evil. Because the American nation, its politicians, and its people have pushed God out of their lives, evil creeps into the void. Evil is not partisan. The godless, secularists of the Left push evil agendas. Likewise, the God-fearing Christian Right often pushes evil agendas.

As a result, the Left, Right, and self-described Christians in all camps put tribal loyalty of party above love of neighbor and love of Christ. And evil advances. It has torn up families, neighborhoods, and communities. It is tearing up the nation.

We need Jesus, not partisanship. Our leaders have failed us on all sides. They've led us to idols and performance art on social media. And like all of humanity throughout history, we, in turn, have defaulted to the original sin.

Back to the Garden

According to the biblical account, God created the first man and woman and placed them as caretakers of a garden. He told them:

> You may surely eat of every tree of the garden,
> but of the tree of the knowledge of good and evil
> you shall not eat, for in the day that you eat of it
> you shall surely die. (Genesis 2:16–17 ESV)

You probably know how this story ends. Our first parents were allowed enjoy the entire garden, and the world for that matter, yet they failed the test. But notice exactly how Satan did it. He promised them something if they ate of the forbidden fruit: "God knows that when you eat of it your eyes will be opened, and you will be like God, knowing good and evil." (Genesis 3:5 ESV)

You will be like God. Satan could have just stopped there, because he had their attention for sure. Right from the start it seems, we were susceptible to the temptation to think we could actually do that—be like God. Ironically, the old-English King James Version translates this statement in a way that really captures the sin in today's context: "ye shall be as gods, knowing good and evil." This core temptation is what got our first parents, and it is what continues to get all of us at some level today.

My friends, don't miss this: The very first entrance of evil into humanity came through this desire to elevate the self to be God. It was an effort to usurp his place in the universe and set ourselves on the throne of all Creation to decide what will be called good and what will be called evil. When you are a god, you can shape reality to your own desires, redefine language to mean whatever you want it to mean, and you are allowed to feel good about all of it. Because that's what gods do.

So, it should not surprise us to see this same desire at the root of the chaos we see in the world today. In other words, the problem itself is not new. It is, in fact, the oldest of problems—disguised as the cutting edge of societal evolution.

When you see it clearly for what it is, everything begins to make sense. Doesn't that describe much of what seems to be chaos in our culture today? Sure, it manifests itself in many different ways, but at the core, the desire remains: to be as gods.

When you understand something, the anxiety lessens, not because the danger subsides but because you realize that what the writer of Ecclesiastes wrote is true: There is nothing new under the sun. Humanity has seen all of this before even if the outer facade has morphed over time. In fact, there has never been a time in human history when this religion has not been present. It is, in fact, the ultimate worship of self as opposed to the worship of a transcendent Creator.

We are seeing it rear its head in yet another form today. I call it the rise of the Religious Left. Think about how much things have changed in our nation in the past ten years, or even just the past five. Our country has not seen this much dramatic cultural change in such a short time outside of the First and Second Great Awakenings. Now there has been another awakening, and it is equally religious. The problem is that it is going in the opposite direction of these previous revivals.

Under the guise of being non-religious, the Religious Left has created a religion fitted with all the trappings of any other religion: hymns, sacrifices, tithes, offerings, sacred spaces, priesthoods, sacraments, eschatology, creeds, confessions, catechisms, and of course, theology.

In the pages to come I answer questions, such as:

- What is this new religion?
- Where does it come from?
- Which challenges lie ahead for us as a culture in dealing with it?
- Beyond just getting angry, what can you do about it?

I promise you that there is a better, more productive path for dealing with this new religion, and that is the gospel. As Pastor Tim Keller explained:

> The gospel is neither religion nor irreligion, but something else entirely—a third way of relating to God through grace. Because of this, we minister in a uniquely balanced way that avoids the errors of either extreme and faithfully communicates the sharpness of the gospel.[6]

There are good reasons to hope for the future, and there are substantive, positive steps we can take. But first, we need to understand what we're up against. In the next chapter, we'll explore how this new religion is really an incarnation of a much older one.

---

6   Timothy Keller, *Center Church: Doing Balanced, Gospel-Centered Ministry in Your City* (Grand Rapids, MI: Zondervan, 2012), p. 85.

CHAPTER 2

THE NEW ANCIENT RELIGION

Why be human when you can be a god?
—Dan Desmarques

Two archeological finds in the 1940s in the Near East gave scholars insight into early Christianity. Scrolls dating from around the time of Christ were discovered in the Qumran caves along the shores of the Dead Sea. This incredible find, preserved for nearly two millennia, would come to be called the Dead Sea Scrolls and includes some of the oldest known complete copies of several Old Testament books. These texts are an archaeological goldmine and helped theologians to confirm the accuracy of modern manuscripts by demonstrating how carefully the Bible has been copied and translated over time. The biblical texts found in

Qumran were consistent with the copies made a thousand years later by medieval monks.[7]

A second significant find was made in December 1945 near the town of Nag Hammadi, Egypt, along the banks of the Nile river, when a group of men uncovered a buried clay jar. One man, Muhammad 'Ali, broke the jar open hoping to find gold or treasure. It was a treasure, but not of gold. What the men found instead was a collection of thirteen leather-bound papyrus books. The codices contained fifty-two Greek texts which had been translated into Coptic, including a passage from Plato's *Republic*. Some scholars believe that they were buried during the fourth century by a local monastery.

Today, the thirteen codices are displayed in Cairo's Coptic Museum. Like the Dead Sea Scrolls, the Nag Hammadi texts have been studied by archaeologists, historians, theologians, and other scholars. However, where the Dead Sea Scrolls contained mostly Hebrew Scriptures or historical texts, the majority of the texts found at Nag Hammadi were Gnostic treatises. The Nag Hammadi library, as the codices are known, includes the only complete copy of the Gospel of Thomas. Because of the Gnostic origin and content of the texts, they are also known as the Gnostic Gospels.

During the 1970s and 1980s several translations of the Gnostic Gospels were published, sparking a renewed interest in Gnosticism and various attempts to harmonize Gnostic teachings with Christianity. The Gnostic Gospels, including the Gospels of

---

[7] Ryan Reeves, "Why Do Christians Care About Qumran and Dead Sea Scrolls?" The Gospel Coalition, February 9, 2017, https://www.thegospelcoalition.org/article/why-do-christians-care-about-qumran-and-dead-sea-scrolls/.

Thomas, Mary, Philip, and Truth, are not included in the sixty-six canonical books of the Bible and are not considered by the Christian church as reliable sources. Why aren't these books accepted alongside the books of the Old and New Testaments? There *are* doubts as to who wrote them and when, but most significantly, the Gnostic message of these books is contrary to the message of Christianity.

What Is Gnosticism?

The roots of Gnosticism go back to the Garden of Eden. In Genesis 3, the Serpent promises Adam and Eve the secret knowledge that God was "keeping" from them. Through this knowledge, Adam and Eve would be like God. Of course, we know how that story ends. We're not God or even like God. We didn't get the promised enlightenment. We got sin, death, and a world of pain and sadness.

Gnostics rejected the biblical account of Creation and the Fall. Instead of a good world created by a good God, they believed everything physical had been made by a lesser, godlike being. The material creation, including human bodies, was thus inherently evil and filled with death and decay. They believed, however, that humans have a divine spark that needs to be set free so that it can be reunited with the One God.

In Gnosticism, humanity's real sin is ignorance, and the path of salvation is through *gnosis* or knowledge. When we have the right knowledge, Gnostics argue, we can be redeemed from the evil, material world. Gnostics embraced strict asceticism, rejecting the physical (food, marriage, sex) to focus on the spiritual. What did the Gnostics believe about Jesus? They taught that Jesus was one of the spiritual guides sent to bring knowledge and enlightenment. They rejected Jesus's incarnation, death, and Resurrection, believing that Jesus only *appeared* to have a physical body.

Christians have been fighting the heresy of Gnosticism since the early church. In the New Testament, St. John argued against Gnostic beliefs that were common in the first century. John's Gospel begins by affirming Jesus's divinity *and* humanity. Jesus is the Word who is God from the beginning. He is the God who created all things. He is also the Word who became flesh and lived with us. Jesus literally had a physical body.

The book of 1 John opens with a refutation of the core Gnostic teachings of dualism, secret knowledge, and enlightenment:

> That which was from the beginning, which we have heard, which we have seen with our eyes, which we looked upon and have touched with our hands, concerning the word of life—the life was made manifest, and we have seen it, and testify to it and proclaim to you the eternal life, which was with the Father and was made manifest to us—that which we have seen and heard we proclaim also to you, so that you too may have fellowship with us. (1 John 1:1–3 ESV)

John was a witness to the realness of Jesus. The Apostles saw Jesus and touched Him. John was also responding to Gnostics who believed that there was some hidden knowledge that humans needed to learn in order to find salvation. John's point was that Christ wasn't hidden. Christ was open to all, and all you have to do is believe in Christ. That's your path to salvation. Historically all Gnostic cults have one thing in common—they suggest society is keeping something hidden from you, and that if you join their group you will have access to that knowledge.

After John died, most Christians had to pivot to take on the heresies that followed, especially Gnosticism. Once the Apostles were gone, false teachers could claim that there was secret knowledge that humans needed to find in order to unlock the meaning of life. To find paradise and eternity, the Gnostics would teach these secret ways.

Christianity went from being a public religion where anyone could read the Bible to gain understanding of God and His plan to redeem humanity to a group of competing cults which each claimed to have access to the hidden truth. They twisted Scripture and Christian beliefs to suit their own advancement. They promised to share their revelation and through this enlightenment people would gain advanced wisdom and eternal life. It appealed to many because it raised them out of average society and drew them into a special few who had insider knowledge that led to heaven on Earth or paradise in the afterlife.

Even as Christians fought diligently to counter Gnosticism, it never really went away. It morphed and subverted itself in new ways. After Constantine became Rome's ruler, Christianity became the official religion in Western society. What do you think happened? All those who were worshiping Zeus five minutes before were suddenly worshiping Christ—not because they had a change of heart, but because they wanted political access to the emperor. That same hypocritical way of living was typical of the rulers of the West. They lived pagan, hedonistic lives while proclaiming Christ on their lips. Christianity became a dominant force in shaping society and culture. While Christianity was started at the fringes of society by a ragtag band of rebels, the "professional" church was allowed more and more access into society to talk to people about Christian faith and morality.

Through the Middle Ages, the Catholic church sought cultural relevance as its influence spread through the vestiges of the former Roman Empire and accommodated local, pagan culture to embrace things that were not compatible with Christianity. The Protestant Reformation brought the church back to the biblical roots and produced a wellspring of accessible knowledge that unleashed Christianity into the masses.

People could read Scripture in their own languages, understand God for themselves, and seek biblical revelation without needing priests to interpret and mediate for them. Because people could read the Bible themselves, they discovered ways the churches at the time had strayed from what the Apostles and early church fathers had taught. The Protestant Reformation also sparked a Catholic Counter-Reformation that forced the Catholic church to go deeper into its theology. Together the two movements improved the Christian church as a whole.

Humanism and the Romantics

During the Enlightenment, philosophers and scholars began to point out the hypocrisy of superficial Christianity. They began to question Christian origins and beliefs and claim that Christianity was appropriating and weaving old, pagan beliefs into the mix. Over time it became more and more possible for people to reject the outward trappings of Christianity and revert to their ancient behaviors, which had been there the whole time.

With the rebirth of pagan humanism during the Renaissance and Enlightenment, a new strand of Gnosticism emerged. *Science* had the secret knowledge necessary for enlightenment. Science told us how the universe was made. Science explained the origin of the species. Science freed us from the superstitions of religion and morality.

Scientific reasoning became the path of salvation from the darkness and ignorance of Christianity. Humanity unencumbered by supernatural beliefs would rise to the pinnacle of human development and achieve utopia. As humanist Isaac Asimov wrote: "Humanists recognize that it is only when people feel free to think for themselves, using reason as their guide, that they are best capable of developing values that succeed in satisfying human needs and serving human interests."[8]

Humanism took the Gnostic idea of the divine spark one step further. Instead of a spark of the divine inside each human being, humans are the center of everything. In humanism, everything revolves around us and exists for our glory. We become gods.[9] With no source of morality outside ourselves, we became our own standard for right and wrong.

The age of Enlightenment almost took the joy out of society. Having gotten rid of the metaphysical and the supernatural,

---

[8] Quoted in Ryan Somma, *Enlightenment Living: Essays on Living a Virtuous Scientific Life* (Ideonexus, 2012), p. 174, https://ideonexus.com/books/.

[9] James Montgomery Boice, "Humanism: You Will Be Like God," Crossway, August 18, 2014, https://www.crossway.org/articles/humanism-you-will-be-like-god/.

everything had to have a scientific explanation. But there was pushback. People wanted to ignore the merely practical or scientific. Where the Enlightenment favored science and reason, Romanticism emphasized emotion, beauty, nature, and individualism.

The Romantics were the hippies of their day. They believed in the inherent goodness of humanity and an idealized natural state free of the constraints of civilization. Unlike the Gnostics, Romantics embraced the natural, physical world. But they did share a belief in enlightenment and the ultimate goal of transformation.

Romantics even adopted the Gnostic idea that the Serpent in the Garden of Eden was bringing truth or enlightenment to Adam and Eve. Romantic poets, such as William Blake and Percy Bysshe Shelley, were intrigued by John Milton's epic *Paradise Lost*, but they saw Satan as the hero of the story. Shelley praised Milton's depiction of Satan: "Nothing can exceed the energy and magnificence of the character of Satan as expressed in *Paradise Lost*."[10]

Twentieth-Century Gnosticism: Hitler and Marx

Gnosticism influenced many of the cultural and political movements of the twentieth century. The connection between political revolutions and Gnosticism goes back to the first-century clashes

---

[10] Percy Bysshe Shelley, *A Defence of Poetry*, quoted in "John Milton's *Paradise Lost*," British Library, https://www.bl.uk/collection-items/john-milton-paradise-lost.

between zealots and the Roman government.[11] If the material, created world is evil, then the political structures and governments of the world are also evil. To free the divine spark within and achieve utopia, the evil order must be overthrown. The revolutionaries had secret knowledge of, or insight to, how to bring about the new, enlightened political order.

The ideology of Nazi Germany was Gnostic at its core, attempting to purify the world of the evil, corrupting influence of the Jews and Jewish religion. The Old Testament God of the Hebrews was pitted against an Aryan "Jesus" and a "positive Christianity." Positive Christianity was neither positive nor Christian. The term was an attempt to baptize and legitimize the Nazi pagan, occult religion. The specifics of positive Christianity and Nazi doctrine were part of the secret, insider knowledge that only the privileged few at the highest levels could understand and define for the masses.[12]

Even Nazi Germany's attempt to take over the world was part of its vision for creating an Aryan utopia:

> Inside the Nazi machine, killing became necessary and one's basic human instinct for sympathy and capacity for judgment had to be repressed or suspended, *because the intensity*

[11] Isaac Ariail Reed and Michael Weinman, "Gnosticism in Modernity, or Why History Refuses to End," *The Hedgehog Review* (Fall 2022), https://hedgehogreview.com/issues/hope-itself/articles/gnosticism-in-modernity-or-why-history-refuses-to-end.

[12] Cunha Alvarenga, "The New Religion of the Swastika Cross," Tradition in Action, translated from *Catolicismo*, September 1971, posted May 15, 2008, https://www.traditioninaction.org/History/G_005_NaziGnostic04.html.

> *of the renunciation of sympathy and judgment*
> *corresponded to the intensity of one's belief in the*
> *radical newness of the world to come.* The secret
> knowledge (Gnosis) of the coming world guar-
> anteed that what seemed immoral now was, in
> reality, the *only moral thing to do*—one had to
> pierce the veil and create, for future generations,
> an entirely new humanity with a new history.[13]
> (Emphasis in original.)

Karl Marx took a similar Gnostic approach. In Marxist ideology, capitalism and the oppressive bourgeois class are the root
of all evil, and the noble proletariat class must be set free. Marx,
and the leaders who followed him, were the keepers of the secret
knowledge necessary for the enlightenment of the proletariat. The
ultimate goal was to implement communism, which would end
the exploitation of the people.

There is no heaven except what we make on Earth; that's
the common thread in modern Gnosticism. World Wars I and
II had a significant role in that development. In the past, wars
were fought across continental Europe. While kings, queens, and
princes played a role, the church would step in to help to alleviate
the suffering of the poor, serving as the medics in the field. With
the world wars, the Red Cross and secular organizations began
to step in and perform charitable roles in place of the church.
Where the church was trying to lead people to God, these secular entities were leading people into reliance on government.

---

[13] Reed and Weinman, "Gnosticism in Modernity, or Why History
Refuses to End."

Creating an interdependent, interconnected civilization where people were tied to these non-governmental entities, such as the United Nations, would bring an end to war. We would have peace for all time.

As the government began to take over social welfare, the church became seen as competition. You don't want people going to the church for help, you want them going to the government for a social welfare program. Many of churches stepped back and ceded ground to government programs because they believed that the politicians were good Christians. Why not allow the government to care for widows and orphans? Over time, government welfare programs created a dependence on a government that never was as Christian as many people in the church believed it was.

From that point, the government took over areas where the church had thrived: adoption, foster care, caring for widows, orphans, the poor, and the hungry. Sadly, the government is far less effective than the church was in caring for physical needs, and without the gospel message, the government can never care for spiritual needs. What we ended up with was an unhealthy dependence on the government as opposed to a healthy dependence on Christ.

Liberal Christianity Arises

As secular organizations and governments took over the social functions that the church had previously provided, offering a new path to "heaven on Earth," churches began to reassess their role in society. In the societal upheaval following World War II, many people had their faith shaken. They needed reassurance. What would the church do in response?

There was a sharp divide within Christianity over what to do. Instead of the church preaching the gospel *and* caring for the widows and orphans, churches emphasized one or the other. Conservative churches became more gospel focused. People needed to hear the gospel and spread the gospel message of hope. Liberal churches, however, focused on the social gospel.

Liberal Christianity had been on the rise since the early 1900s. Liberalism combined the scientific rationalism of the Enlightenment with the ethical relativism of the Romantics. The central goal of liberalism was accommodating Christianity to the new secular age. Like earlier humanists, liberals rejected the supernatural and miraculous elements of Christianity. They denied Jesus's virgin birth, His miracles, and His bodily Resurrection. They had little use for the strict, moralistic Old Testament God. Instead, they taught a message of a pacifist, socialist Jesus whose life was an example for us to follow. As Richard Niebuhr summarized, "A God without wrath brought men without sin into a kingdom without judgment through the ministrations of a Christ without a Cross."[14]

J. Gresham Machen, a conservative theologian in the early 1900s, wrote about theological liberalism in his book *Christianity and Liberalism*: "The chief modern rival of Christianity is 'liberalism.' An examination of the teachings of liberalism in comparison with those of Christianity will show that at every point the

---

[14] H. Richard Niebuhr, *The Kingdom of God in America* (New York: Willett, Clark & Company, 1937), p. 193.

YOU SHALL BE AS GODS

two movements are in direct opposition."[15] As Machen pointed out, liberal Christianity, instead of trying to bring people to paradise, was trying to bring eternal paradise to Earth. Adherents of liberal Christianity believed that only they could save the world and bring utopia here. The result was that liberal churches went out into the culture to feed the poor and administer their false gospel message. Conservative Christians ceded cultural influence to try to save souls. Even Hollywood preached the message of good Christians as benevolent, kindly liberals, opposed to narrow-minded, bigoted evangelical conservatives.

The Bible seems very clear that we're supposed to share the gospel *and* care for the needy. But with the split of the church, it turns out the people who cared for the needy physically were deeply persuasive to many people about how they should live, work, and build society. Meanwhile, the secular Left took over public education, teaching children the humanist, relativist, Gnostic religion of Self.

The priests of this religion were able to co-opt government schools because in the 1950s and '60s, the Supreme Court[16] decided that atheism was the opposite of religion and not a religion in itself. While the U.S. Constitution says the government will not establish a religion, the government in fact did establish a type of religion by embracing secularism.

---

[15] J. Gresham Machen, *Christianity and Liberalism* (New York: The MacMillan Company, 1923), p. 53.

[16] See *Abington School District v. Schempp*, 1963, https://supreme.justia. com/cases/federal/us/374/203/.

Postmodern Gnosticism

Toward the end of the twentieth century, postmodernism emerged as the leading philosophy in Western civilization. Postmodernism emphasizes self and personal experiences. There are no absolutes. Truth is whatever you believe it to be. Religious beliefs are personal, and religious practice is individualistic. In fact, many people today like to say that they are "spiritual, but not religious."

New Age spirituality and religious practices incorporate elements of ancient religions. What's old is new again. Healing crystals replace household idols. People consult Ouija boards and mediums to connect with the spirit world. Some take drugs for enlightenment and transcendence.

Spirituality is self-focused in our postmodern age. The goal is to improve yourself, soothe yourself, and be true to yourself. In this postmodern ideal, we are our own truth. *I'm* never the problem. *You're* the problem because you have your truth, and I have my truth. And when our truths are incompatible *you* are the heretic, not me. We've created a god in our own image, and that image is Self. As Carl Trueman explains in *The Rise and Triumph of the Modern Self*:

> An overriding desire for inner personal happiness and a sense of psychological well-being lie at the heart of the modern age and make ethics at root a subjective discourse. Human beings may still like to think they believe in good and bad, but these concepts are unhitched

from any transcendent framework and merely reflect personal, emotional, and psychological preferences.[17]

Whatever your truth, you can find an "expert" to support your point of view. Nowadays every cultural-sociological movement has a medical doctor and a scientist with a Ph.D. to form the basis of its claims. There are doctors who promote the idea that vaccines cause autism. There are scientists claiming that having children is "scientifically proven" to harm the environment, and so smaller families are a moral obligation. Some doctors will tell you that life does not begin until a child exists outside of the womb. Others will tell you that it is scientifically possible for a boy to become a girl.

Language then tracks the political consensus of the scientific community. And it is a political consensus. Secular liberals have worked very hard to co-opt cultural institutions so that, regardless of truth, science reflects opinion instead of the other way around. The two-parent heterosexual nuclear household may have been, for thousands of years, the most stable way in which to raise children, but get a bunch of liberal sociologists masquerading as scientists together in a room and soon they'll tell you science says that the two-parent heterosexual nuclear household is bigoted, white supremacist, and part of the patriarchy.

Gnostic influence is especially clear in our cultural obsession with identity. Our identity comes from within and is subjective.

---

[17] Carl R. Trueman, *The Rise and Triumph of the Modern Self: Cultural Amnesia, Expressive Individualism, and the Road to Sexual Revolution* (Wheaton, IL: Crossway, 2020), p. 88.

Instead of being created in the image of God, male and female, you get to create yourself in your own image and decide whether you're male or female, black or white. Rachel Dolezal identified as a black woman, even though biologically, she's white. Ellen Page was born biologically female, but because her internal identity is male, Ellen is now Elliot, which makes the movie *Juno* deeply confusing.

Caitlyn Jenner always was the truth behind Bruce Jenner. In the mind-numbing logic of "gender conformity," Caitlyn was always there just waiting to be revealed. According to the new Gnosticism, Rachel, Bruce, and Ellen freed themselves from the external, material world and found their true selves in the internal, spiritual world.

Gnosticism also manifests itself in radical environmentalism. Christianity teaches that God created nature and that we are to be stewards of it. With environmentalism, we go from controlling nature so that we flourish to controlling ourselves so that nature flourishes. We've elevated creation above the Creator, and we have to some degree put ourselves lower than creation.

Instead of the church teaching morality to curb sin, the government regulates our behaviors to protect the environment from our ecological "sins." That's not the language it uses, but in the environmental religion, sin is anything that causes problems for the planet, either in commerce, in trade, or in human stewardship of the environment. The government replaces God, and instead of giving us the Ten Commandments, it gives us a fifty-book U.S. code to modify our behaviors and teach us how we're to live, along with an even more voluminous Code of Federal Regulations to get even more specific.

We've overpopulated the Earth, we have too many mouth breathers, breathing carbon dioxide, driving their trucks. We need to silence and punish anyone who doesn't embrace this new theology. They are heretics whose lives must be destroyed, chased off the airwaves. And, oh, by the way, the whole world is going to burn and end unless you hold your breath and don't release any carbon dioxide.

We have a new inquisition, and you see it everywhere you look. Whether it's punishment on social media if you don't buy into transgenderism, or losing your home and business for sinning against the environmentalist religion, it's going to get worse. As people leave Christianity, and Christianity leaves this nation, we don't get new religions, we get old ones repackaged to appear new. Just like those old religions sacrificed people to their gods, we're going to see the environmentalists who lead this new religion become some of the most violent. After all, they are the high priests, and they do not want to make their goddess Greta Thunberg scowl at them.

Gnostic Wokeism

Two possessed men cried out to Jesus. The demons spoke and Jesus asked them their names. "Legion, for we are many," they told Him. Then, knowing that their fate was sealed, the demons begged the Lord to cast them into a herd of pigs running by instead of being cast into the abyss. Christ did, and the pigs ran down the hill into the water and drowned.[18]

But the demons didn't die.

They got out of the pigs and were bored. So, they invented social media.

One of the only upsides to Twitter, now called X, is that we occasionally get glimpses of the intellectual elite and realize that they are pretty damn stupid. Thus, we come to Nikole Hannah-Jones, a woman whose sole existence is to tell the members of the white patriarchy that they will be absolved of their own racism by giving her money. Nikole Hannah-Jones, of course, gets paid by white wokes to rewrite American history into something sinister, racist, and bad. Hannah-Jones has a history of making assertions based on propaganda and proclaiming that facts are propaganda.

Hannah-Jones and others like her are just various forms of L. Ron Hubbard selling a modern Gnosticism to rich, white wokes who need Jesus, but don't believe in Him. They promise secret enlightenment if only you'll throw money at them, buy their books, and give them tithes. They will open your eyes and reveal the true history, the true nature of racism, and the true depths of depravity in America that are so woven through our systemic injustices that they'll never be undone—so long as the money keeps flowing.

Rich white people who feel a sense of shame or guilt about their positions seek absolution for their sense of guilt. The race hustlers then simultaneously assuage their guilt and perpetuate the shame to keep the money rolling in. It is no longer these white

---

[18] This section was previously printed here: Erick-Woods Erickson, "The Race Hustling Gnostics of White Guilt Absolution," Substack.com, November 12, 2021, https://ewerickson.substack.com/p/the-race-hustling-gnostics-of-white.

wokes who are to blame, but the systems. And systems are controlled by others who are not as enlightened.

It is no coincidence that as the United States has seen its first black president, first black vice president, a black man representing South Carolina in the Senate, and scores of other prominent non-white leaders across the country, the Gnostics of race have grown louder and more vocal. They sense their gravy train disappearing as America moves beyond its past sins.

There is a ready market for rich secular progressives always looking for special insight, better knowledge, and absolution for their feelings of guilt. These Gnostics can be applauded for grabbing this guilt and steering it toward race with supposed special insight.

L. Ron Hubbard offered Xenu, volcanoes, DC-8 spaceships, and thetans to explain the guilt of success to the dimwitted Lilliputians of Hollywood. Gnostic woke leaders have offered America's past to explain the guilt of current success to rich wokes.

Gnosticism is on the rise in our culture, among political liberals and conservatives. People believe that if you read certain websites or listen to certain voices, you can gain insight to the world and a deeper knowledge of what's really happening around you.

The same thing is happening in the discussions on race and social justice. On both sides of the debate, people say, "Hey, I've got the hidden knowledge the media isn't telling you about. I've got the hidden knowledge the Republicans or the Democrats aren't telling you about." Inevitably some fringe, malcontented group—whether white nationalists or Antifa—wants the malcontented souls to come in and believe that it has access to a "truth" that is not publicly available.

The false gospel of Gnosticism has been a problem in the Christian church since the beginning. In fact, the "new" progressive religion of the Left isn't new at all. It may seem like it came out of nowhere, but what we're seeing today is the latest incarnation of an ancient heresy.

The Christian Response

There's a story that C.S. Lewis was once asked by a group of religious scholars, "Is there anything that really separates Christianity from the other religions?" In response, he offered one word: "Grace."

Christianity is truly unique. It combines mercy—not getting what you deserve, with grace—getting what you don't deserve). Others will argue that their religions have these concepts, but when you dig deep, it's always conditional. With Christianity, the only condition is to accept Christ. It doesn't matter how bad you are. If you accept Christ and repent, you get forgiveness and eternal life.

There is no concept of that in secular Gnosticism. There may be mercy, they might spare you from what they think you deserve. But in their world, you can't receive things you don't deserve because secularism is premised on a zero-sum game. There is a finite number of resources. Some give, some take. But grace is unacceptable. You can't give people something they don't deserve. As a result, there's an unbridled level of hostility. And ultimately, everyone has to keep moving further and further to the left to stay ahead of the mob. Eventually we'll all fall off the cliff. As liberal standards and norms evolve over time, even someone who's in a perfect position today will suddenly find himself a sinner who can't be redeemed. With a big enough public sacrifice, he might find a measure of mercy, but there is no grace.

You can put up a windmill or a solar panel, buy a battery car and a bike, it won't save you. Even if you're doing everything possible to save the planet, you're still screwed. As long as the guy next door has a bunch of kids and drives an SUV that uses gas, the planet is doomed. There's no grace in these systems, and this is where we are in our society.

By the way, don't think it doesn't affect political conservatives. There are many political conservatives who are abandoning authentic Christianity for something that looks and sounds like Christianity. These are people who employ the rhetoric of Christianity who have no idea of the concept of loving your neighbor or extending grace to someone who lets you down. It's a cultural Christianity where culture should *look* like Christianity, but we really don't want Christianity itself. In the same way, QAnon is Gnosticism for some on the Right.

People are buying into these Gnostic ideas. It's affecting our politics. It's affecting our judgment. It's affecting our decision-making. It is particularly dominant right now on the Left. Those on the Left have abandoned the real church for one of their own creation. They have stopped worshiping the real God for the creation that God made.

Across North America and Europe, environmentalists force conversions to their faith by requiring you to turn off your power, starve, and freeze in the wintertime. You will be made to pay for their Gnostic god. And if you do not submit to their god, you will be persecuted and punished.

Christianity has the only answer to the problems of this world. The problem is that we've forgotten our mission of spreading the gospel. Oh, we're very missional in the sense of wanting to go to Mexico or Africa. Just like the empires of the 1500s and 1600s, we're sending the missionaries off to conquer territory and Christianize the world. But we've forgotten the people in our own backyard who are craving Christ.

We have the opportunity for local churches to return to Jeremiah 29 and seek the welfare of the cities in which they are because there they'll find their welfare. We're seeing a Protestantism in this country that for so long felt itself so dominant, it did not have to stick to the basics. It could refine itself into political theater and combine itself into a megachurchopolis, packing people into a building on a Sunday, without caring about the people down the street from the church on a Monday.

We've embraced a live-and-let-live attitude with the fallen culture around us. We've embraced plurality and are attempting to "coexist." That coexistence can creep into our house and we're not even aware of it. Parents are abdicating their responsibility to raise their children as Christians, whether it's to a school or to a church program. Mom and Dad are so busy making money to provide for the family that they've neglected the souls of their kids.

CHAPTER 3

THE JUDEO-CHRISTIAN VACUUM: ACCOMMODATION AND COMPROMISE

*The greatest menace to the Christian Church
to-day comes not from the enemies outside, but
from the enemies within; it comes from the
presence within the Church of a type of faith
and practice that is anti-Christian to the core.*
—J. Gresham Machen

The world is invading the church and bringing politics with it. My denomination, the Presbyterian Church in America (PCA), has been debating how to respond to the controversy that started a few years ago when a group met in a PCA church and held a conference called "Revoice" on how to minister to same-sex-attracted individuals. Revoice made waves for what seemed to be an attempt to normalize unbiblical sexual identities behind biblical veneers.

Since then, there have been many well-meaning attempts to bridge an apparent divide between the church and the big cultural issue of the day—sexual ethics. We're living in an age where Christians need to speak boldly as culture clashes with our values. Many would argue that this is all needlessly controversial and blame Christians for picking fights.

In reality, orthodox Christianity is on the defense here.

We didn't pick the fight. But we must respond.

Silence and obsequiousness in language where Scripture speaks plainly is self-defeating.

Like the Christian church in Nazi Germany, the church today has compromised, and is accommodating the culture. Author Francis Schaeffer sounded the alarm in 1984 with his book *The Great Evangelical Disaster*:

> There is only one word for this—namely accommodation: the evangelical church has accommodated to the world spirit of the age. First, there has been accommodation on Scripture, so that many who call themselves evangelicals hold a weakened view of the Bible and no longer affirm the truth of all the Bible teaches—truth not only in religious matters but in the areas of science and history and morality.... [S]econd, there has been accommodation on the issues, with no clear stand being taken even on matters of life and death.[19]

---

[19] Francis A. Schaeffer, *The Great Evangelical Disaster* (Wheaton, IL: Crossway, 1984), p. 37.

Accommodation and compromise within the church has created a Judeo-Christian vacuum allowing the new Gnosticism to step into the void left behind. You see it manifested in a whole litany of things, from non-evangelical mainline denominations embracing gay-pride flags and "diversity" to PCA pastors writing a book in favor of reparations for slavery.[20] There's also overwhelming use of words like "relevant" and "relevance" and attempts to be relevant to culture. But going back to the founding of the faith, Christianity has always been counterculture. It drew people to the faith by not reflecting the culture around it but by standing against it. It's the epitome of relevance because it looks different from the world.

As discussed in the previous chapter, the liberal church moved away from upholding biblical morality and ethics, and toward a social gospel. Even in the evangelical church, there has been an emphasis on metrics and the mechanics of growth. The thinking seems to be, "Well, we must have so many people in the door. We must share the gospel with so many people. We must feed so many people. We must hit these numbers to stay relevant and have a voice."

It should come as no surprise that when your main focus is trying to bring people in the door instead of sharing the gospel and changing lives, the result is a church that looks more and more like the culture around it. After all, you can't afford to offend people, or you'll scare them off.

I see greater and greater antagonism in society toward Judeo-Christian values because the church has failed to do what it

---

[20] Duke L. Kwon and Gregory Thompson, *Reparations: A Christian Call for Repentance and Repair* (Ada, MI: Brazos Press, 2021).

should have done. Once it allowed the government to take over many of the core functions of the church, like caring for widows and orphans, the government was able to take over the position of influence that the church once had in the public square.

Secularists are gaining dominance in society, and they are increasingly antagonistic toward Christianity. I don't think you'll get to the point of Christians killed in the streets of North America like we see in some Muslim parts of the world. But I do think we're going to see many more people driven from their jobs because of their faith. As more people revert to Gnosticism, many more people will be silenced in the public square. In the society being built, it'll be the Christians who have to be the quiet citizens. And the church has only itself to blame.

The nation is in a spiritual crisis, and the church is too distracted by politics to deal with the broken souls who need Jesus. Marriages and families are collapsing. Children are unneeded, unwanted, disposable, and inconvenient. Society is collapsing, and Christians have accommodated, compromised, and abdicated. Why make time for broken people, when what the world really needs is Christian affirmation of reparations, a book tour on NPR stations about the post-Trump Christian Right, and the nodding agreement that the church is filled with white privilege and racists?

The nation has no answers for what is going on. An increasingly godless society cannot regulate and legislate its way out of this mess. *O church, arise. You're missing your moment.* As J. Gresham Machen wrote, "The Church is the highest Christian answer to the social needs of man."[21] The world needs the church, our nation needs the church, we need the church.

But we need a *faithful* church, not a compromising one.

The State of the Church

> *The grace of God is rejected by modern liberalism. And the result is slavery—the slavery of the law… It may seem strange at first sight that "liberalism," of which the very name means freedom, should in reality be wretched slavery. But the phenomenon is not really so strange. Emancipation from the blessed will of God always involves bondage to some worse taskmaster.*
> —J. Gresham Machen

Liberal Christianity is spreading in our churches, and it's coming from seminaries and church leaders. A survey of churches in mainline denominations in Canada revealed a growing divide between congregants and pastors in many denominations. Overwhelmingly, the laity surveyed believed in miracles, that God hears prayers, that the Resurrection is real and physical, and that

---

[21] J. Gresham Machen, *Christianity and Liberalism* (New York: The Mac-Millan Company, 1923), p. 159.

the Bible is the word of God. Conversely, the pastors and priests believed none of those things.[22]

In the American church, conservative denominations may squabble on some theological points, but they all believe these basics. The progressive, mainline denominations, if not yet dead, have given up the game to culture altogether. Thankfully, while I think there are some in my own denomination who lean too far Left, on the whole, across the spectrum of pastors, they're all Bible-believing Christians. They differ mainly on how to speak biblically to the present culture. But even that shared theological ground doesn't stop the infighting.

My big frustration right now is with theologians and pastors who have taken to Twitter, now X, to build followings and pick fights. It just isn't healthy. It does, however, mean gaining followers, so many keep at it, leaving a trail of carnage and division in their wake. There is even organized bullying among Christians, some of whom operate as if they're in a political campaign. In conservative denominations, anyone who brings up racial reconciliation is called "woke" or an advocate of the racist and Marxism-inspired critical race theory (CRT), even when he isn't. The Twitterati have lost all nuance and sense.

Tim Keller, a pastor in my denomination, wrote one of the best critiques of CRT out there.[23] I have referred thousands of

22 Douglas Todd, "Instead of Gretta Vosper's Atheism, Clergy Choose Alternative Views," *Vancouver Sun*, June 10, 2016, https://vancouver-sun.com/opinion/columnists/douglas-todd-instead-of-atheism-canadi-an-clergy-choose-alternative-views-of-god.

23 Timothy Keller, "A Biblical Critique of Secular Justice and Critical Theory," *Life in the Gospel*, undated, https://quarterly.gospelinlife.com/a-biblical-critique-of-secular-justice-and-critical-theory/.

people to his critique, which specifically shows how CRT is not compatible with Christianity and will not lead to true racial reconciliation. But the fringe on social media has repeatedly attacked Dr. Keller, claiming that he's a proponent of CRT. Why? Because he thinks the church needs to address racial reconciliation, and he willingly engages with those with whom he disagrees. And he does so civilly.

Dr. Keller told me a while back that since we are all made in the image of God, we all have something to share with others, even when we disagree. There's wisdom there not often found on social media. But who needs nuance when you can expand your platform by being either an "uncompromising absolutist fundamentalist who condemns anyone who disagrees" or an "accommodating culturalist who condemns anyone who has biblical standards." Frankly, the people who think the church needs to look just like the world, and the people who think the church needs to look nothing like the world, are *both* wrong.

Some Christians take a different approach to the issues of the day. Instead of duking it out online, they try to avoid conflict by not addressing hot-button topics. There is a pervasive commercialism even within evangelicalism where churches may be somewhat countercultural, but they're still really hinged in culture. Pastors become more like dynamic motivational speakers than preachers. They are to make people feel good about themselves and not challenge them too much about morality and biblical ethics. Make the experience good and they'll keep coming back.

Even pastors who preach through Scripture and aren't trying to be culturally relevant on the news of the week tend to avoid difficult subjects. Instead of giving their congregations pastoral leadership on these issues, they say, "We're not going to address transgenderism, abortion, or the culture clashes around us, because it's not relevant to the Scripture we're scheduled to discuss this week." And they're very careful to pick books of the Bible that never touch on those subjects.

Between the motivational pastors with big Instagram followings and fancy sneakers, and the pastors who want to avoid all controversial topics, the church is failing to live up to its purpose of making disciples. Jesus was very clear that believers will be persecuted, as He was. Sadly, a vast array of churches in this country sells a gospel that says, "You can be a comfortable Christian and never have to worry about persecution." But that's contrary to the gospel Jesus preached. We don't need to try to offend people—when Christians share the gospel and don't conform to society, people *are* offended. We can't avoid uncomfortable discussions just so no one ever gets mad at us.

As we discussed in the previous chapter, liberalism and the new Gnosticism are religions without grace. But don't think these aren't influencing political conservatives, too. There are many political conservatives who are abandoning authentic Christianity for something that looks and sounds like Christianity, even using the rhetoric of Christianity, but has no concept of grace or loving your neighbor. It is a Christless Christianity that wants culture to *look* Christian but that really wants nothing to do with Jesus and authentic Christianity.

Gnosticism, especially the claims to special, insider knowledge, is making inroads in churches on both sides of the political spectrum. Social media, of course, makes it easier for people in our postmodern culture without objective truth to embrace this new Gnosticism by following individual celebrities to access their special knowledge.

The Left uses "science" to claim more than two genders exist. Members of the Left twist facts and demand that everyone agree with them, use their language, and adopt their pronouns. Distortion of reality is cropping up on the Right, too. Consider some news sources on the right that claim to have special insight on COVID-19 and vaccines, as well as on satanic pedophiles attempting to implement a new world order. There's even a strain of atheism among these people embracing guys like James Lindsay, a renowned atheist.

Even some of the churchgoing conservatives are walking away from church and putting their faith in politicians like those on the Left. Without any apparent sense of irony, conservative Christians put their faith in a multi-divorced serial philanderer, who has shown no yearning for redemption, to protect them from the Left. Progressive Christians put their faith in the godless world around them to protect them from persecution. On both sides, Christians have become transactional. The conservative ones think it was worth it because the U.S. Supreme Court overturned *Roe v. Wade*, while progressive Christians so crave approval by the world that they can't celebrate a possible end to abortion for fear of losing the approval.

It's all transactional, yet neither side will admit it. Both the Right and the Left are wrapped up in the same spiritual crisis, and so few in the church will even address it.

Next, I discuss evidence of the church's accommodation and compromise on sexuality, transgenderism, abortion, environmentalism, and racism.

ERICK ERICKSON

Cultural Accommodation on Sexuality

At the beginning of this chapter, I mentioned the controversy in the Presbyterian Church in America over the Revoice conference. Some inside the PCA made excuses for pastor Greg Johnson whose church hosted the original conference a few years ago. Let's fast forward to today. Revoice is still meeting, and things have gone exactly as predicted:

> During the conference's two-hour lunch breaks, Revoice offered "affinity groups," broken into various categories: gender minorities, family/ loved ones of LGBTQ+, bisexuals/pansexuals, asexuals/aromantics, women "assigned female at birth," mixed-orientation heterosexual marriages where one spouse remains same-sex attracted, and celibate partnerships where those who are same-sex attracted but celibate live together. In Side B circles, those are called "spiritual friendships." Other affinity groups were categorized by race: BIPOC for black or indigenous people of color and AAPI for Asian American or Pacific Islanders.[24]

This story is only one of many attempts to weave the spirit of the age into Christianity, just as the Gnostics tried in the early church. Progressives and liberals have been compromising on biblical sexual ethics for years. Influential authors and public figures

---

[24] Mary Jackson and Todd Vician, "Identity Crisis," *World*, October 21, 2022, https://wng.org/articles/identity-crisis-1666367393.

like Rachel Held Evans and Jen Hatmaker have promoted cultural accommodation by joining the ranks of "affirming Christians." Evans wrote:

> If you're a gay, lesbian, bisexual, transgender, or queer reader, I hope you already know you don't need my affirmation to live whole and joyful lives, just as God made you. You are beloved children of God, and there is nothing I or any other Christian writer or church leader can say to alter that.[25]

Lutheran Pastor Nadia Bolz-Weber's book *Shameless: A Sexual Reformation*, was her attempt to undermine traditional Christian teachings on sexuality. In it, she defends abortion, homosexuality, sex outside marriage, divorce, and pornography as healthy, godly expressions of sexuality of which people should not be ashamed. In an interview promoting her book, she explained her own experience with divorce and extramarital sex:

> So what happened was, I get divorced, like the most amicable divorce you can imagine.... I get together with my boyfriend and start having sex and...it felt like an exfoliation of my whole spirit. I'm like, "This is so good for my brain chemistry, and my body, and my heart." ... [W]hy in the world would the Church say "Don't do this"?

---

[25] Rachel Held Evans, "LGBTQ+," https://rachelheldevans.com/blog/lgbtq, October 8, 2019.

Like I could tell it was what I needed, and it
was so good.[26]

Many Christians share Bolz-Weber's views on casual sex.
Hook-up culture has become increasingly common in singles
ministries and college ministries,[27] even at Christian colleges.[28] As
a 2020 Pew Research poll found:

> Half of Christians say casual sex—defined in the
> survey as sex between consenting adults who
> are not in a committed romantic relationship—
> is sometimes or always acceptable. Six-in-ten
> Catholics (62%) take this view, as do 56% of
> Protestants in the historically Black tradition,
> 54% of mainline Protestants and 36% of evan-
> gelical Protestants.[29]

Even the issue of same-sex marriage has gone from fringe to
majority acceptance in recent years. Many mainline Protestant

[26] Kevin Garcia, "Making Sex Shameless, w/ Nadia Bolz-Weber," "A Tiny
Revolution" Podcast, Dec. 31, 2018, https://www.listennotes.com/pod-
casts/a-tiny-revolution-kevin-garcia-2OwX6G5o0LV/.

[27] Mary DeMuth, "Loving Jesus & Hooking Up," MaryDeMuth.com,
March 19, 2015, https://www.marydemuth.com/hooking-up/.

[28] Carrie Dedrick, "Can I Be a Casual-Sex Christian?" Crosswalk.com,
updated March 23, 2015, https://www.crosswalk.com/blogs/chris-
tian-trends/can-i-be-a-casual-sex-christian.html.

[29] Jeff Diamant, "Half of U.S. Christians Say Casual Sex Between Consent-
ing Adults Is Sometimes or Always Acceptable," Pew Research Center,
August 31, 2020, https://www.pewresearch.org/fact-tank/2020/08/31/
half-of-u-s-christians-say-casual-sex-between-consenting-adults-is-
sometimes-or-always-acceptable/.

churches now regularly perform same-sex ceremonies. The arguments among Christians in favor of supporting homosexuality and same-sex marriage tend to focus on biblical themes of love and compassion. They claim Jesus never spoke about homosexuality, and we should be careful not to take the Bible too "literally." Often the debate is couched in terms of justice and righting past wrongs:

> An ever-growing number of Christian clergy and lay people now believe that rejecting gay civil rights because of a literal adherence to certain verses directly contradicts these themes. They point out how these views are hurting all of the church, especially its most vulnerable members: young gay people who are convinced that their very essence is sinful. Furthermore, they can no longer support unjust laws that penalize committed same-sex couples and their families.

> As more and more church members thoughtfully and prayerfully confront the evidence, it will only be a matter of time before the majority of Christians of all stripes become allies rather than antagonists for justice and equal rights for gay people. Then we will come out on the right side of history once again.[30]

And who wants to be on the wrong side of history?

---

[30] C.S. Pearce, "The Christian Case for Gay Marriage," *Los Angeles Times*, December 2, 2012, https://www.latimes.com/opinion/la-xpm-2012-dec-02-la-oe-pearce-christianity-gay-marriage-20121202-story.html.

Cultural Compromise on Abortion

Christians have been part of the pro-life movement from the beginning of the church. In the first century, A.D., Roman Christians rescued babies left out to die on trash heaps. The church has historically sought to protect life from womb to tomb.

Abortion is often an emotionally charged topic, and like the current debates over sexuality, Christians have a tendency to be swayed by emotional arguments. The arguments attempt to tug at our heartstrings over poor women who are being forced to have babies they don't want and can't afford. And if they don't have access to legal abortion on demand at every stage of pregnancy, they'll die in back alley abortion clinics. Women at pro-abortion protests are dressing up like characters from *The Handmaid's Tale*, comparing restrictions on abortion to a dystopian fantasy where women are forced to be surrogates.

In liberal and progressive churches, the compromise over abortion has reached unimaginable levels. Pastors in some mainline denominations argue for abortion as a moral good. Rev. Carlton Veazey, president of the Religious Coalition for Reproductive Choice, said:

> The right to choose has changed and expanded over the years since *Roe v. Wade*. We now speak of reproductive justice—and that includes comprehensive sex education, family planning and contraception, adequate medical care, a safe environment, the ability to continue a pregnancy

and the resources that make that choice possible.
That is my moral framework.[31]

If you aren't familiar with the Religious Coalition for Reproductive Choice, its website explains that it is "a multifaith, intersectional, and antiracist movement for reproductive freedom and dignity leading in spiritual companionship, curating frameworks for faith leaders, and training the next generation of activists."[32]

Another organization, Just Texas, promotes "Reproductive Freedom Congregations." Just Texas was started to fight pro-life and other conservative legislative policies in Texas and end silence and shame around abortion:

> Too often, congregations—even progressive faith communities—perpetuate a conspiracy of silence around reproductive health issues, especially abortion. This silence can make people reluctant to share their experiences or reach out for support, for fear of being shamed, judged, or stigmatized. We are here to say abortion is a blessing.[33]

---

[31] "Pro-Choice Does Not Mean Pro-Abortion: An Argument for Abortion Rights Featuring the Rev. Carlton Veazey," Pew Research Center, September 30, 2008, https://www.pewresearch.org/religion/2008/09/30/pro-choice-does-not-mean-pro-abortion-an-argument-for-abortion-rights-featuring-the-rev-carlton-veazey/.

[32] Religious Coalition for Reproductive Choice, https://rcrc.org/.

[33] Just Texas, "Reproductive Freedom Congregations," https://justtx.org/rfc/.

Pastor Jes Kast from the United Church of Christ serves on the clergy-advocacy board of Planned Parenthood. She defends her position on abortion as faithful to Christianity:

> I believe reproductive rights and bodily auton-
> omy are deeply important. I believe that is faith-
> fulness to Christianity. I believe in access to
> safe and legal abortions. I believe every person
> I encounter, including myself, has the right to
> their body. When that bodily autonomy is taken
> away, to me, that is against Christian scripture,
> and is against the Gospel I believe in.[34]

Abortion is a blessing? Being against abortion is contrary to the gospel? That's news to generations of Christians.

There are even organizations that offer resources for celebrating abortion including hymns, sermon prompts, calls to worship, and other liturgical elements. From "A Ritual for Reproductive Choice":

> I light the first candle for those whose story
> includes the choice to end a pregnancy. The
> circumstances vary, the timelines of our lives are
> diverse, but each and every end is also a begin-
> ning, and so I light this candle for all who have
> aborted a pregnancy or partnered someone [sic]

---

[34] Emma Green, "A Pastor's Case for the Morality of Abortion," *The Atlantic*, May 26, 2019, https://www.theatlantic.com/politics/archive/2019/05/progressive-christians-abortion-jes-kast/590293/.

in an abortion, for whatever reason, under whatever circumstance.

May the flames of these candles and the many stories they represent remind us of the fire of commitment we carry inside, to ensure that all people have freedom and agency over their reproductive choices, and that reproductive justice is upheld as a fundamental right for this and future generations.[35]

When the Supreme Court overturned *Roe v. Wade* in June 2022, you would have expected Christians to be celebrating. Some were, but it was stunning to see many other Christians lamenting the possible end of abortion in the U.S. Laura Ellis, project manager for Baptist Women in Ministry, wrote:

Overturning Roe does not support life. This week, like many of you, I'm wholly disheartened by the refusal of safe and affordable access to reproductive health care that will most harshly affect society's most marginalized women. As Christians we must try our best to create conditions for each other that are more human, more grace-filled and more hospitably Christ-like. In tandem with my faith, I hold to the belief that

---

[35] Julia Hamilton, "A Ritual for Reproductive Choice," Unitarian Universalist Association, September 27, 2021, https://www.uua.org/worship/words/litany/ritual-reproductive-choice.

illegalizing abortion will not create these kinds
of conditions.[36]

It wasn't too surprising to see mainline, liberal denominations come down in favor of abortion. They've been doing so for
decades now. But when Baptists are decrying the overturning of
Roe, you realize how far the compromise has gone.

Worshiping the Environment

In Genesis, when God placed Adam and Eve in the garden, He
instructed them to tend and keep it. After they sinned, their
descendants took two basic approaches toward Creation and the
bounty around them. Some destroyed and laid waste to the land
while attempting to become wealthy and powerful, hoarding natural resources and misusing the gifts God had given them. Others
looked at the world, nature, and animals and decided to worship
them instead of the God who created them.

Whether they admit it or not, today's environmentalism is a
secular religion with creeds, forms of worship, and eschatology.
The path to salvation in radical environmentalism is not based
on the individual, but on society as a whole. While my salvation
is through putting my faith and trust in Jesus, the secular environmentalist believes the world is going to end because of climate
change. Unless we collectively change our ways, we will all die.
This is why we are going to see more violence in the environmental

---

[36] Laura Ellis, "Why I'm a Pro-Choice Christian and Believe You Should
Be Too," *Baptist News Global*, May 6, 2022, https://baptistnews.com/
article/why-im-a-pro-choice-christian-and-believe-you-should-be-too/.

movement. Dissenters like you and me are preventing society as a whole from achieving salvation, and we must be stopped.

Christians should be good stewards of the Earth and our resources, and many are. However, within our churches, there is a growing movement attempting to appease radical environmentalists on the Left. Even Pope Francis, in his 2015 letter "Laudato Si': On Care for Our Common Home," wrote about the need for "an ecological spirituality grounded in the convictions of our faith."[37] In it he stated that people need an "'ecological conversion,' whereby the effects of their encounter with Jesus Christ become evident in their relationship with the world around them."[38] Such ecological spirituality "is not an optional or a secondary aspect of our Christian experience."[39]

The Catholic Church recently intervened to end mining operations in the Philippines. From the statement released:

> We believe that the project would not serve
> the overall interests of the province and would
> pose a threat, particularly to the lives and lands
> of the communities on the island, and the rich
> biodiversity in the area. We feel *a moral duty*

[37] Pope Francis, "Laudato Si': On Care for Our Common Home," The Holy See, May 24, 2015, p. 62, https://www.vatican.va/content/francesco/en/encyclicals/documents/papa-francesco_20150524_enciclica-laudato-si.pdf.

[38] Ibid.

[39] Ibid., p. 67.

to safeguard and uphold the well-being of our shared environment.[40] (Emphasis added.)

People in England and Wales are demanding that the Church of England divest from fossil fuels. A group called Christian Climate Action provides a list of ways how churches can participate in the "Church Divestment Day of Action." These include holding a prayer vigil or staging a "die-in" to represent the deaths caused by climate change.[41] The group also has prayers you can download. Here is an excerpt from "Prayer for an End of the Fossil Fuel Era":

> As we undergo an ecological conversion, we ask that this pain transitions to hope as we endeavor to find new ways to rectify our transgressions.
>
> We pray in earnest for a "Just Transition" from fossil fuels to more sustainable energy sources; a better future, whereby, our biosphere, nature and humanity are at the centre of the energy transition....

---

[40] Ferdinand Patinio, "Church Groups Call for Halt to Mining Ops in Romblon," Philippine News Agency, February 6, 2023, https://www.pna.gov.ph/articles/1194462.

[41] Christian Climate Action, "Church Divestment Day of Action: Sunday 5th March 2023," January 14, 2023, https://christianclimateaction.org/2023/01/14/church-divestment-day-of-action-sunday-5th-march-2023/.

Strengthen us to take care of the individuals and communities who will bear the undue burden from the transition to a green economy.

We trust in you O Lord. You are with us, working in us and through us. All things will be made new.[42]

Ambrose Carroll, Ph.D., is a pastor and the founder of Green the Church, "a sustainability initiative designed to tap into the power and purpose of the Black Church Community and expand the role of churches as centers for environmental and economic resilience."[43] Carroll teaches "green theology" and hosts revival tours including "a night of worship, vegan meals, and days spent discussing environmental injustices and opportunities with clergy and activists."[44]

Some churches have accommodated environmentalism to the point of crafting worship services around the annual Earth Day. The Presbyterian Church (U.S.A) has resources for Earth Day or other "Creation Care Worship Services." It also provides materials, such as sermon prompts, liturgy, and calls to action, from

---

[42] Diocese of Kilmore, "Prayer for an End of the Fossil Fuel Era," undated, https://christianclimateaction.org/2023/01/14/church-divestment-day-of-action-sunday-5th-march-2023/.

[43] Green the Church, "Our Mission," https://www.greenthechurch.org/our-mission.

[44] Jeneé Darden, "One Pastor's Mission to Fight for Environmental Justice Through the Black Church," *Everyday Health*, February 3, 2023, https://www.everydayhealth.com/black-health/one-pastors-mission-to-bring-environmentalism-to-the-black-community/.

Creation Justice Ministries "to equip faith communities to protect, restore, and more rightly share God's creation."[45]

Creation Justice Ministries, formerly known as the National
Council of Churches Eco-Justice Programs, suggests bulletin
inserts or handouts with steps or products that congregations can
use to make their home "green." The featured resource is a hand-
out on the wilderness:

> The wilderness is deeply woven into Christianity
> and other faith traditions. They [sic] were cen-
> tral to the spiritual journeys of Moses, Jesus and
> Muhammad. This new resource will help us in
> our modern day efforts to reflect peacefully and
> reconnect with the Creator through study, wor-
> ship and congregational action.[46]

Another downloadable resource, "Save Our Sacred Seas,"
calls for Christians to care for the ocean as "a sacred gift from
God."[47] And, here are some elements from a liturgy provided by
the Unitarian Universalist Association:

> From the Call to Worship: "Today we join
> together to hold our hope and our pain, to

---

[45] Presbyterian Mission, "Earth Day Sunday: Celebrate Earth Day Sunday or Other Creation Care Worship Services," https://www.presbyterian-mission.org/ministries/environment/earth-day-sunday/.

[46] Creation Justice Ministries, "Creation Justice Resources: Educational Resources for All Ages," https://www.creationjustice.org/education-al-resources.html.

[47] Creation Justice Ministries, "Save Our Sacred Seas," https://secure.everyaction.com/B4ijJfOGY0izmVvGkImu0g2.

honor Earth, and to recognize how deeply our relationship with Earth and our work for environmental justice is intertwined with ALL of our spiritualities."

The homily: "'The Children Take Action!—A Climate Change Story' by Seema Deo and Kylie Jayne. This illustrated children's story is about a group of kids on a Pacific Island who learn about global warming and do their own small part to help stop it, and save their island."

From the Prayers of the People: "We join together as many and diverse expressions of one loving mystery: for the healing of the earth and the renewal of all life."

A Seed Ritual: "Instead of centering our worship around a sermon, today I invite you to plant a seed to honor our connections with Earth and with communities around the world."

A closing ribbon ceremony: "We may need to commit to new ways of acting in this world, or in our religious communities, or to appreciating Earth as part of our spirituality, or to something else. Only our hearts know to what we need to commit ourselves."[48]

Does this make you sick to your stomach? It should.

My friends, God alone is worthy of worship, and no amount of compromise on our part will make secular environmentalists like us. Christians and the church will always be treated as enemies preventing them from achieving their utopia.

Racism: Blame Shifting and Finger Pointing

Here's the painful bottom line—a great many churches and leaders are in search of a new idol to worship. They're done with the gospel. They'll dabble in critical theory and convince themselves that they can co-opt Marx and pick and choose what works. Let me be clear: Racism is a sin that is real. The church can and should work to stamp it out. But it has to be done with the gospel, not by dabbling with Marxism-originated ideas. Opposing racism is the Christian thing to do. But some churches are going down a dark road of accommodating secularists to placate them.

Frankly, many pastors in evangelicalism have embraced Trumpism, to their eternal shame. In response, many who have opposed Trumpism are embracing whatever they perceive is contrary to Trumpism. That involves shouldering the burdens of secular racial reconciliation at the expense of the gospel and Christian racial reconciliation.

---

[48] Diana Smith, "Earth Day Worship Service," Unitarian Universalist Association, July 4, 2017, https://www.uua.org/worship/words/complete-service/earth-day-worship-service.

Just as some pastors want to be known as "with Trump," some want to be known as "not with Trump," and so they stand with the loudest voices against him, denouncing racism and marching in the streets. Instead of preaching Jesus, they're spending all their time talking about race.

Race has been a relevant cultural issue in the past year, and we should want the shepherds to address current issues and examine how the gospel can deal with them. But we should be mindful that many of the loudest voices in the church right now on race issues are people who have chosen to remain silent about abortion and biblical sexual ethics. If a shepherd of Christ's flock can't be bothered to speak about those targeting Christians, and Christian schools and businesses being harassed to change policies on transgenderism, marriage, and abortion, we should not waste our time listening to them. Those are the men most likely chasing their idols, not professing the gospel.

In my own denomination, the Presbyterian Church in America, some of the very same pastors who embraced Revoice have unsurprisingly embraced critical race theory. The overlap is not surprising at all. After all, a hallmark of postmodernism is that words no longer have fixed definitions, and that reality is shaped by words. They'll take the words of the gospel and give each word a new meaning.

An example of redefinition is found in a recent article on the intersection of Christianity and racial justice. "In this article," the authors state, "we intend to address the intersection of grace and race. While we use social and racial justice interchangeably, we define social justice as a focus on racial identity and justice as it relates to Christian faith."[49]

The Racial Justice Institute redefines what it means to be one in Christ:

> Christians are called to be one in Christ (Galatians 3:28), not to erase the beautiful differences the Creator bestowed upon humanity, but to utterly destroy the hierarchies and domination that humans attach to those differences.[50]

The Black Lives Matter movement made significant inroads in churches. Jemar Tisby, founder of the Reformed African American Network, said, "What Black Lives Matter did was highlight the racism and white supremacy that still has a stranglehold on much of white Christianity. You have this phrase and this movement that is forcing people, essentially, to take sides."[51] The United Church of Christ has a position statement on "Why 'Black Lives Matter,'" which encourages churches to join the Black Lives Matter movement:

---

49 Sharia Brock, Angelica Hambrick, and Alexander Jun, "The Intersection of Christianity and Racial Justice Advocacy," *The Journal of the Association for Christians in Student Development*, Vol. 15, No. 15 (2016), p. 25.

50 "Racial Justice Institute," *Christians for Social Action*, https://christiansforsocialaction.org/programs/racial-justice-institute/.

51 Quoted in Eliza Griswold, "How Black Lives Matter Is Changing the Church," *The New Yorker*, August 30, 2020, https://www.newyorker.com/news/on-religion/how-black-lives-matter-is-changing-the-church.

When a church claims boldly "Black Lives Matter" at this moment, it chooses to show up intentionally against all given societal values of supremacy and superiority or common-sense complacency. By insisting on the intrinsic worth of all human beings, Jesus models for us how God loves justly, and how his disciples can love publicly in a world of inequality. We live out the love of God justly by publicly saying #BlackLivesMatter.[52]

Some Christians have even joined in the call for reparations. The National Council of Churches has partnered with Harvard University in the "Journey to Jubilee" campaign "for reparative justice and democracy reform through racial healing and transformation."[53]

Pastor Thabiti Anyabwile, who was born Ron Burns, changed his name when he converted to Islam. "Many African Americans are being drawn to Islam by a black nationalist ideology. I thought I'd be a Muslim the rest of my life and commit myself to black nationalist causes." When he returned to Christianity, he didn't change his name, "For me, it wasn't as much a Muslim name as a cultural association. Thabiti has its roots in Africa, a Swahili

---

[52] United Church of Christ, "Why 'Black Lives Matter,'" https://www. ucc.org/what-we-do/justice-local-church-ministries/justice/faithful-action-ministries/racial-justice/justice_racism_black_lives_matter/.

[53] National Council of the Churches of Christ in the USA, "Journey to Jubilee: Campaign for Reparative Justice and Democracy Reform," https:// nationalcouncilofchurches.us/anti-racism-resources/reparations/.

word suggesting, 'a true man and upright.' Anyabwile is Arabic and means, 'God has set me free.'"[54]

Anyabwile wrote in favor of reparations: "Reparations are simply the biblical principle of restitution taught throughout Scripture applied to the specific history of slavery and the descendants of slaves in America."[55] Pastor Peter Jarrett-Schell's recent book *Reparations: A Plan for Churches* argues that white denominations, like his own Episcopal church, must pay significant reparations for their participation in racism:

> Nothing less than the soul and integrity of the Episcopal Church is at stake. This debt is owed for the benefit the church has received from four hundred years of participation in anti-Black racism. It should be paid, not only as a matter of moral imperative, but also for its potential to help break the Episcopal Church from the gilded shackles of white supremacy that have defined our history.[56]

Like we saw with churches worshiping the environment, some churches offer resources for worship services celebrating Martin Luther King, Jr. One resource from the Presbyterian Church (U.S.A.) includes:

[54] Rob Wilkins, "Thabiti Anyabwile: Grace Across the Divide," *Outreach Magazine*, June 8, 2020, https://outreachmagazine.com/interviews/11446-thabiti-anyabwile-grace-across-the-divide.html.

[55] Thabiti Anyabwile, "Reparations Are Biblical," The Gospel Coalition, October 10, 2019, https://www.thegospelcoalition.org/blogs/thabiti-anyabwile/reparations-are-biblical/.

[56] Peter Jarrett-Schell, *Reparations: A Plan for Churches* (New York: Church Publishing Incorporated, 2023).

A Prayer of Confession: Most Holy and merciful God: we have condemned racial injustice in our pronouncement, yet we cling to the privileges derived from social inequalities. All too often we are blind to our complicity in maintaining systems of oppression and deferring the hopes and dreams of the oppressed for freedom. Give us the courage to name our sin, give us the strength to claim responsibility for our actions. Give us the grace to pay the price for changing our behavior.

Responsive Reading: I have a dream that the Holy Spirit will arouse in me that very flame of righteousness that caused Martin King to become a living sacrifice for the freedom and liberation of all God's Children. Then I will be able to resist racial injustice everywhere I see it, even within myself.[57]

The problem with churches engaging with racism on the theological front is simple—the United States demands a separation of church and state. The answer to systemic racism is the gospel of Jesus Christ. The United States will not accept that answer. Therefore, churches are left to do what exactly? Work with those on the Left who reject Christianity to enact public policy solutions that are devoid of Jesus and implemented by people who do not view racism as sinful, per se, but as an opportunity to exert power?

---

[57] Presbyterian Peacemaking Program, "Martin Luther King Jr. Day Worship Resources," https://www.presbyterianmission.org/wp-content/uploads/mlk-resources.pdf.

Good luck with that. This is not to say churches should abandon the cause. I think churches just have to go about it differently.

Transgenderism: The Latest Cultural Compromise

As mentioned earlier, a number of prominent evangelicals went silent after *Roe v. Wade* was overturned. While many evangelicals were vocal, some of the prominent ones were silent. The same has been true for the advance of transgenderism in our country. Prominent evangelicals, particularly female members of the church with platforms, have not spoken out about the issue. As girls see boys come into their ranks, one might think that would provoke a response. But from too many, it has not.

As these two acts of silence speak loudly, some politicians who wear their supposed Christianity on their sleeves—from President Biden to the "Reverend" Raphael Warnock to Nancy Pelosi—are pretty adamant that life begins at some point, but they are not guided by their faith to decide when a child lives or dies.

Many of the same politicians have become comfortable with genital mutilation. They insist that parents accept their children's sexual orientation and be prohibited from trying to change it. But parents must also accept their children's transgender identity and must permit them to be changed. It is a deeply contradictory madness, and sadly many Christians and churches are going along with it.

Rachel Held Evans argued that the gospel is good news for those who do not conform to gender binaries and even called traditional beliefs on gender a false gospel:

The gospel of Jesus Christ is not so fragile as to be unpinned by the reality that variations in gender and sexuality exist, nor is it so narrow as to only be good news for people who look and live like Ward and June Cleaver. This glorification of gender binaries has become a dangerous idol in the Christian community, for it conflates cultural norms with Christian morality and elevates an ideal over actual people.[58]

Austen Hartke, a graduate of Luther Seminary, founded the Transmission Ministry Collective for transgender Christians. As a transgender person, Hartke's goal is to reconcile the Bible with transgender ideology. In *Transforming: The Bible and the Lives of Transgender Christians*, Hartke writes, "God created me with a body that was designated female...and with a mind that identifies as male.... I don't think God made a mistake. I think God made me transgender on purpose."[59]

That theme is common in transgender-affirming churches and resources for Christians. God didn't make a mistake in giving transgender people bodies and minds that don't match up:

[B]eing transgender does not mean that I was born in the wrong body. Being transgender means that God has placed me in the body that looks like one gender while I identify as being

---

[58] Rachel Held Evans, "The False Gospel of Gender Binaries," November 19, 2014, https://rachelheldevans.com/blog/gender-binaries.

[59] Austen Hartke, *Transforming: The Bible and the Lives of Transgender Christians* (Louisville, KY: Westminster John Knox Press, 2018), p. 2.

another. It is neither right nor wrong… When a Christian says that being transgender is a sin or an abomination, they are really trying to tell God that He made a mistake and that flies in the face of all that they say they believe. Since we do not understand why God made a person transgender, who are we to question?[60]

Churches and clergy from different denominations have been making changes to welcome and include transgender people. Rev. Hannah Wilder wants her Episcopal church to be open to everyone and emphasizes a message of love: "I would love it if St. Mary's was known as the gay church, where queer and transgender people can feel welcome here. The church needs to change or it will die and for good reason, because nobody wants to be excluded. That was Jesus's message—to love all."[61] A message of love includes everyone, even those who disagree, right? Well, maybe not *everyone*.

Saint David of Wales Episcopal Church in Portland, Oregon, has added signs that you can use whichever bathroom you prefer.

---

[60] Katie Leone, "God Made Me Transgender, and God Does Not Make Mistakes," Believe Out Loud, https://www.believeoutloud.com/voices/article/god-made-me-transgender-and-god-does-not-make-mistakes/.

[61] Julie Gallant, "New Priest at St. Mary's Episcopal Church Brings Message of Love and Acceptance," *Ramona Sentinel*, January 18, 2023, https://www.sandiegouniontribune.com/ramona-sentinel/news/story/2023-01-18/ramonas-new-reverend-hannah-wilder-begins-sharing-ideas-about-love-and-acceptance.

It also includes preferred pronouns on church name tags and refers to "siblings in Christ" and not sisters or brothers.[62]

Rebel and Divine is a congregation of the United Church of Christ. Most of the people who attend are at-risk youth who don't feel welcome elsewhere. One member of the congregation was interviewed in an NPR article. Katrinna "was raised a strict Southern Baptist and a boy in a conservative, religious town in rural Kentucky," and "felt it was religion that kept her mother from fully embracing [her]." She says Rebel and Divine is the only place she feels comfortable as a 23-year-old Wiccan.[63]

The Church of England has even issued guidance on how to use the rite of Affirmation of Baptismal Faith to celebrate gender transition: "The Church of England welcomes and encourages the unconditional affirmation of trans people, equally with all people, within the body of Christ, and rejoices in the diversity of that body into which all Christians have been baptized by one Spirit."[64] Bishop Julian Henderson, chair of the House of Bishops Delegation Committee, said:

---

[62] Deena Prichep, "Trans Religious Leaders Say Scripture Should Inspire Inclusive Congregations," NPR, September 25, 2022, https://www.npr.org/2022/09/25/1124101216/trans-religious-leaders-say-scripture-should-inspire-inclusive-congregations.

[63] Stina Sieg, "Pastor Redefines 'Church' for Transgender Youth," NPR, February 21, 2016, https://www.npr.org/2016/02/21/467243382/pastor-redefines-church-for-transgender-youth.

[64] News release, "Guidance for Welcoming Transgender People Published," The Church of England, November 11, 2018, https://www.churchofengland.org/news-and-media/news-and-statements/guidance-welcoming-transgender-people-published.

We are absolutely clear that everyone is made in
the image of God and that all should find a welcome in their parish Church. This new guidance
provides an opportunity, rooted in scripture, to
enable trans people who have "come to Christ
as the way, the truth and the life," to mark their
transition in the presence of their Church family
which is the body of Christ. We commend it for
wider use.[65]

Every person on the planet is made in the image and likeness
of God. Because of that, we can learn from everyone, even as we
might disagree on some, most, or all issues. As so many churches
and Christians are accommodating and compromising with liberalism and the secular, pagan, Gnostic religion growing out there,
we need to engage more, not less. We should encourage engagement as a missional and evangelical exercise of principled conservative ideas. In the next chapter, I discuss the inevitable conflict
between Christianity and the Gnostic religion of the Left.

---

[65] Ibid.

CHAPTER 4

CULTURES IN CONFLICT

And they are enraged at us when we speak thus
about their gods, though, so far from being
enraged at their own writers, they part with
money to learn what they say; and indeed the
teachers of these authors are reckoned worthy of
a salary of the public purse and other honors.
—St. Augustine, *The City of God*

The population declined. Global temperatures rose. Inflation hit 15,000 percent over the course of one hundred years. The migration of people from destabilized regions increased. Wind and solar energy supplied the planet with all its power. Food was becoming scarce. And infrastructure seemed to be failing across the nation.

On September 4, 476, Romulus Augustus stepped down from the throne of the Western Roman Empire after generations of ineptitude, ideological idolization, and incompetence undermined the foundations of Rome. And the Church was in the midst of a doctrinal crisis as the world entered what is often called the Dark Ages.

This period is often credited as ending around the year 800. But for half a millennium, the world experienced stagnation, lawlessness, riots, military conflicts, new religions, and the return of old ones. It took centuries for Rome to fall. Centuries of people not caring, looking the other way, keeping their heads down, and abandoning the Great Commission to retreat to monasteries. In short, the Dark Ages were the result of a period of neglect.

Now, 1,022 years after the end of the Dark Ages, as populations decline, temperatures rise, global inflation is on the rise, and people move restlessly about the planet, environmentalists are plunging the world into the first phase of a new dark age of wind and solar dependence.

Like many of the gods in the secular pantheon, "Mother Earth" is seen as totally dependent on their chief god—us. They foresee the world as burning unless they gain exactly what they want as a sacrifice from their neighbors. Ironically, much of what environmentalists claim is climate change turns out to be the result of inept, corrupt, and inefficient policies—often pushed by progressive politicians.

California did us the courtesy of writing the prelude to this new dark age, with its blackouts and mass energy strain, because it prioritized moving to wind and solar power instead of prioritizing power grid infrastructure upgrades and baseload power. The state's power suppliers could not cover the costs of keeping their power lines in good condition lest they be fined for not moving fast enough to "clean energy." To save Mother Earth, the state returned to windmills, the occult, and even looked to the stars in the hopes that Tom Cruise and Will Smith would be able to summon aliens to help them. Of course, not everyone in secularism thinks that E.T.s will be their saviors. New York Representative Alexandria Ocasio-Cortez had the brilliant and original idea of sacrificing cows in order to save the planet.[66]

The reality, however, is that today's environmental policy is inherently Malthusian,[67] the idea that food and energy production will never be able to keep up with the human population. We saw this idea as Rome declined, and we are seeing it again today. The usually unspoken premise of this movement is that humanity must suffer for the planet to survive. *We need to save the planet! There must be fewer of us on Mother Earth, and those who survive must live in more miserable conditions.* As we saw in the previous chapter, churches across the world are starting to buy into this neo-Gnosticism. They submit to the secularist liturgies, prayers, and need to end human life to save the planet.

Many progressives will object to claims that what we are seeing is a failed policy or ideology, but few will see or hear their objections in the darkness to come. There will either not be enough power, or it will be too expensive for anyone to tweet about it.

Wind and solar power are not baseload power. Baseload power is power that can be flipped on as demand rises. Wind and solar farms are inefficient power sources, fully dependent on the

---

[66] Alexandria Ocasio-Cortez, H.R. 109, Recognizing the Duty of the Federal Government to Create a Green New Deal, 116th Cong., 1st sess., 2019, https://www.congress.gov/bill/116th-congress/house-resolution/109/text.

[67] Thomas Malthus, *An Essay on the Principle of Population and Other Writings* (United Kingdom: Penguin Books Limited, 2015).

wind blowing and the sun shining. While environmentalists claim that batteries can store excess power to use when wind turbines do not spin and the sun does not shine, there is not enough lithium nor enough batteries to meet the demand.

The Lights Begin to Dim

In Europe, the continent moved so quickly away from its baseload power to renewables that it increased its dependence on Russia for natural gas. Now some Europeans are freezing to death because of the continental embrace of the environmentalists' demands.[68] Power is being rationed. It will only become more expensive. There will not be enough of it. It is starting, and for nothing.

Instead of investing in nuclear power, the Europeans rejected it for a dystopia where they get to pay Putin for his war in Ukraine, which helps the Chinese with their proxy war against us, which increases the need for the Chinese to enslave Muslims to work in their lucrative lithium mines. Which is also why the Chinese keep backing cartels and corrupt Pink Tide movements in Latin America so they can get their hands on even more lithium, which is not great for the environment anyway. It is bad no matter how you slice it.

On the opposite side of the world, California's power grid is under an incredible burden. In triple-digit heat, people turn off their air conditioners and lights to avoid straining the system. A week after California mandated that new vehicles in the next

---

[68] Brittany Raymer, "100,000 People Expected to Die This Winter in Europe Due to Green Energy Policies," John Locke Organization, December 23, 2022, https://www.johnlocke.org/100000-people-expected-to-die-this-winter-in-europe-due-to-green-energy-polices/.

decade must all be electric, the state insisted that people either unplug their cars or use gas generators to charge them. California has fewer than 600,000 electric cars, and they are already too much of a strain on the existing power grid. The state does not have enough land for the solar and wind farms needed to supply the power needed to convert California's thirty-eight million vehicles to battery power. But, you may be thinking, at least the batteries in the cars are manufactured ethically and give people more jobs. And you would be right, as long as you don't think about the fact that the majority of the lithium for these batteries are also from China's mines powered by—wait for it—slavery. (But Communist China argues it can't be slavery because the Uyghurs are not people *per se*.)

The very environmentalists who demand we use these energy sources would balk at the idea of building a solar or wind farm in an area that could possibly threaten an endangered species. Better to have human beings castrated, raped, beaten, and killed than having Bambi and his pals adjust or move. These environmentalists begin their gatherings by thanking indigenous tribes for the land where their events take place (but don't offer to return the land) and demand reparations for an institution that ended a century and a half ago. They seek to be "washed" from the societal sins committed by people who were dead long before they themselves were born.

In the past century, we have seen incredible growth through nuclear power programs across the world. They could even be credited with maintaining the international status quo and keeping us all from World War III. But while China is planning to build six to eight nuclear power plants a year until 2035, we are planning to paint a brighter tomorrow using all the colors of the wind.

Rome became an unserious nation. We are quickly becoming unserious people here, too.

If the United States does not begin an immediate expansion of its nuclear energy base load capacity, what is happening in California will spread nationwide. What is happening in Europe will become the norm in America. We will enter a new dark age. And only Communist China will benefit, because the Chinese regime does not care which gender you list on your Twitter profile, so long as you bow to its national personality cult.

Their "Truth" Goes Marching On

If you think that energy is the only place where the secularists are willing to damn our nation with their premonitions of doom, think again. It is not a coincidence that, just as superstitions grew in the prelude to the Dark Ages, sophist thinking and superstitions are spreading now. The Americans embracing their inner chakras and healing crystals and who think men can get pregnant are the loudest voices of environmental lunacy. They envision themselves as the Creators and will create a hell on Earth backed by pseudo-science and screams about climate change to cover their sophistry and incompetence. People will die, and it is entirely preventable.

The power going out in America is a choice. It is a choice that too many progressives are making and imposing on everyone. According to their worldview, they must be the saviors, or no one will. They are the masters of their own destinies. Their worldview does not allow dissent or heresy. It must reign supreme. The environment must be preserved. No matter the cost.

Like John Maynard Keynes' infamous book, *The End of Laissez-Faire*, many now openly advocate killing other human beings because they might be disabled, poorer, older, younger, or cost more to keep alive than a hamster. Eugenics parades itself under the title *quality of life* to persuade people that grandma's dementia, your baby's potential autism, or the potential for poverty means a person "shouldn't be forced to live this way." The same people who advocate the dissection babies, making comatose women surrogates for gay men, and ending the lives of the elderly are the same people who demand allegiance to Mother Earth.

This is evil. Pure and simple.

As Rome fell, the cults returned. They mixed with the cults of the Visigoths, Goths, and more. And the leaders of the Christian faith had to come to terms with this theological counter-attack. They went out to the places where the Romans abandoned their infant children who were born with deformed legs, sensory issues, or were just unwanted. They rescued those children and showed them Christ's love. Today, Christians must step up once again. As Proverbs says, "Rescue those who are being taken away to death; hold back those who are stumbling to the slaughter."

The Volumes of Silence

I am increasingly alarmed by how many prominent evangelicals went silent after the *Dobbs v. Jackson's Women Health* ruling. That case killed *Roe v. Wade*. It was something all Christians and most conservatives had been advocating for, for almost fifty years. While many evangelicals were vocal, some of the prominent ones were not.

The same was true when President Obama did his infamous 180° on the mandatory legalization of homosexuality. It was when the BLM riots overtook many people's genuine concerns over equality and police reform in 2020. It is true during the despotic march of transgenderism in the country. Many prominent evangelicals have not spoken very loudly about the issue, if they speak at all.

On the abortion and transgender issues, I have noticed that evangelical women, specifically, drop the ball as they try to keep their images politically clean. The acts of silence from these "leading" ladies speaks loudly. There are loud voices in the church who stand on the political Right, which have been insisting that it is a sin to vote for the Democratic Party because this party now openly advocates abortion on demand and embraces genital mutilation.

Stacey Abrams advanced the argument during her second failed gubernatorial campaign in Georgia. She said that abortion is not just a women's healthcare issue, but an inflation issue. If you can't afford groceries, you cannot afford a baby. Journalist Mike Barnacle had asked Abrams to move on from abortion to "kitchen table issues" and she went there. Barnacle did not follow up with the obvious implication—if you cannot afford groceries and you cannot afford a baby, why must a baby live after birth? A child three weeks removed from the womb is just as helpless and dependent and even more costly than a child three minutes from being removed from the womb.

What did we hear from pastors across the nation? *Crickets.*

The Democratic Party has become comfortable with more than just abortion. It now advocates genital mutilation. One must be prohibited from sending one's gay child to a camp that tries to make the child straight, but one must also be prohibited from keeping one's child from genital mutilation. Parents must accept that their gay child is gay and be prohibited from trying to change the child. But parents must also accept that their son is a girl and the child must *be encouraged* to change. It is a deeply contradictory madness, and the leadership of an entire political party is advancing it.

I'm hard pressed to think a Christian in good conscience can vote for a party whose leadership advocates such barbarism. But then I'm hard pressed to answer the Christian who points out the way Republicans keep funding Planned Parenthood—the priests of Moloch. The GOP is pro-life, but funds the sacrifice. Many Republican leaders are opposed to restrictions on genital mutilation, too, yet the majority of the party in Congress codified gay marriage. This gets icky, sticky, and contradictory for those who want to deal with more than the partisan talking points.

But then there's another partisan point. Where are the evangelicals who say you cannot vote for the party of abortion?

We can all call out the prominent evangelicals for their silence on the end of *Roe* and their silence on the advance of transgenderism. But many of the very same voices who will call out those prominent evangelicals for their silence are themselves silent about this happening on the Right. How can we seek to find a solution in a culture where all roads inevitably lead to Rome and the pagan cults headquartered there?

Pax Romana

The answer is a lot simpler than some of the organizations constantly asking for your money would like you to believe. America is like Rome. It always has been intentionally similar. Let me explain.

The Roman Republic was founded in 509 B.C. after the rural Romans overthrew a tyrant to ensure their freedom from oppression. Obviously, this freedom was not identical to what we see in the world today, but it was similar. The Republic had legislative, executive, and judicial branches of government and promoted private property and respect of one's neighbors. It grew and grew until it covered the Mediterranean and most of Europe.

It has been said that if a contemporary person were dropped in the Roman period, he would have most of the amenities he enjoys today: running water, air-cooled housing, heating vents throughout the home, a productive interstate system, and waste management. There were also stadiums for local sporting events, currency and free markets, vacation resorts, and park systems. Medicinally, the Romans also had gyms, doctors, hospitals, and sanitation, and bathing and hair care were the norm.

The Republic maintained its course for about two hundred years before Julius Caesar took over. After a civil war concluded and he was assassinated, the state entered a period of reform under Octavian (Augustus), Caesar's great nephew and adoptive heir. From then on, the Roman Empire (though many still called it the "Republic" at the time) began an era of top-down control, where the experts made all the decisions with the input of the priesthood of the cults.

But something went wrong under Augustus.

In the boonies of Israel, a miracle happened. Jesus Christ was born to a virgin named Mary, and He was ordained the Messiah that Judaism had been waiting for since the Adamic, through the Noahic, Abrahamic, Mosaic, and Davidic covenants. He preached a gospel of reconciliation between God the Father and sinful humanity. To open the personal relationship, He submitted Himself to Rome's corruption and was crucified unjustly to save an unjust people who despised the thought of not being their own salvation. In so doing, He changed the world three days after His death by rising again and building His church.

Rome was never the same again, and neither was the world.

Within a single generation, Christianity spread throughout the Roman Empire and offered an alternative from worshiping the state, idols, or flesh. The visible City of Man was being openly challenged by the invisible City of God. Emperors came and went, tried the most horrible forms of persecution and tolerance steeped in heresy, but the Word of the Lord stayed the same and outlasted them all. Secret attempts, public attempts, personal attacks, and more could not overcome the spiritual conflict occurring within Rome.

The Pax Romana (Peace of Rome) was the Roman sense of peace through strength. If Caesar held power and squashed his rivals, then the state was at peace. Anyone who encouraged slaves to revolt, or tried to depose the gods would also be silenced. But as Rome fell into anarchy, the Romans noticed their Pax Romana was falling apart as the deified emperors continually fell from power, regime after regime after regime.

What stood in contrast to the decaying system? Christians.

Sometimes the brave and courageous outspokenness of Christians had dramatic impacts on Roman society. Christian martyrs and mentors influenced generations of Romans as the slow decline took place. Church history began to form as people like Telemachus championed the abolition of gladiatorial games, where slaves would fight and kill one another for public amusement. But he and others were also sacrificed and silenced for their audacity to question the way Rome was governed.

Others in the education system, such as the former professor of rhetoric (then the equivalent of legal studies) Aurelius Augustine, otherwise known as Augustine of Hippo, taught a new philosophy counter to Roman stoicism. Augustine had lived the Roman dream and had everything he could desire: a girlfriend, great job, vast amounts of money, respect, and influence in every religious and philosophical pool in Rome. But after a radical personal conversion, he gave it all up, married the mother of his son, and pursued a calling in ministry. He was a child of Grace and lived this truth.

From Augustine's greatest work we gain the imagery of the world being divided by two cities: a City of Man and the City of God. As Rome cascaded into oblivion in the fifth century, the Christians had no fear. They respectfully continued their abstinence from the ways of the City of Man (which was demonstrated in the corrupt, lewd, and evil character of the city of Rome). Through this change in perspective many people continued pursuing their vocations but as converts, and not as coveters. But most important, Augustine reminded the Christians of his day that their world was in a state of conflict.

The Secret Conflict

Right now, in schools across the country, the next major political revolution is under way. I know it sounds dramatic, but when you look at the facts it is pretty evident. Except that the priesthood of this cultish revolution does not want to acknowledge it. It is happening at the most influential levels of society: the education bureaucracy.

Adolf Hitler, in the summer of 1933, said, "If the older generation can not get accustomed to us, we shall take their children away from them and rear them as needful to the Fatherland."[69] The Communist Bolsheviks of the Soviet Union coined a term for this educational exercise in universal conformity in 1917: "political correctness." In both cases, subjects were expected to toe their respective party lines to weed out those who were not loyal enough to either personality cult.

Isaiah Berlin wrote a series of essays on how the Soviets strengthened their position by shutting parents up and going after the vulnerable minds of their kids. Today, the Left is doing the same with your kids. But for now, its members are largely operating in secret and trying to ignore the stories when they get caught.

In Maryland, a recent story emerged as a mother named Kristy Rush uncovered what her daughter's "involvement" meant at the aptly named "Gender and Sexuality Alliance" club at Chesapeake High School.[70] In the videos and messages that Rush uncovered, a man calling himself a transgender teacher founded a club where he and his students could, "carry on, be gay, and start a revolution."

This guy also sent messages to the kids in this club encouraging them to call him "mom," and under school policy had his

---

[69] Adolf Hitler, speech on June 1933, https://nla.gov.au/nla.obj-533446278/view?sectionId=nla.obj-580935500&partId=nla.obj-533493132#page/n13/mode/1up

[70] Libs of TikTok, "Private DMs, Scantily Clad Students, and Police: Meet the Trans Teacher Who Has Parents Alarmed," November 2, 2022, https://www.libsoftiktok.com/p/private-dms-scantily-clad-students.

room designated as a "safe space" for these kids to go to during any class or period if they requested it. Parents were not informed but became suspicious when the club published a series of posts showing a new school policy of punishing faculty and students who used "deadnames" (birthnames) and failed to use last names for inclusivity, and punishing faculty "if [a student] believes a teacher is purposely ignoring homophobic, transphobic, or bigoted behavior in the classroom."[71]

The situation has only escalated as Rush pulled her daughter out of the school after finding videos on her daughter's phone of students engaging in sexual acts in this "safe space." She then began alerting other parents about what was going on, only to have the teacher file a Peace Order with the District Court to shut her up. Now this teacher continues to encourage LGBT protesters to chant outside Rush's home until his disciple is taken from her parents and returned to him. Oh, and he also told all the protestors to read aloud the names of the other students' parents as a warning that this could and would happen to them if they pulled their kids from his class.

This is not an isolated incident. In New York, an elementary school teacher was caught by the mother of the child referring to a nine-year old girl as "Leo," and using exclusively "he/him pronouns."[72] The parents only discovered any of this when the

---

71 Ibid.
72 Claudia Aoraha, "New York Teacher 'Manipulated' Fifth-Grade Student Into Changing Gender Without Parents' Consent," *Daily Mail*, February 23, 2023, https://www.dailymail.co.uk/news/article-11804089/New-York-teacher-manipulated-fifth-grade-student-changing-gender-without-parents-consent.html?ns_mchannel=rss&ns_campaign=1490&cito=social-twitter_mailonline.

little girl had drawn a suicidal image saying, "I want to kill myself." When the parents asked their daughter if she identified as a boy, she said she absolutely did not, but her teacher said she was a boy. The parents have since sued the school for manipulating their daughter and discovered that the teacher had been reading from multiple books on gender theory to her class of nine-and ten-year-olds.

The teacher had not been removed after telling her students to "try being gay" nor after multiple physical abuse investigations. And the school refused to notify parents that their children were being coached not to tell their parents what they learned. The school then, "looked into it," which only resulted in the young girl being placed in another classroom and the teacher staying in her original position. The girl has since been bullied extensively by other students as her teachers do not even know which pronouns to use when referring to her.

In Florida, a teacher at Howard Middle School in Orlando conducted a little ceremony with his students for Black History Month to teach them critical race theory.[73] He then videoed the event and it went viral.

> The video follows three black girls entering the room, where one white student awaits to remove a sweater for one black student as all three sit down in chairs arranged in a row. Behind them,

---

[73] Darlene McCormick Sanchez, "Teacher on Leave After Video of White Students Bowing to Black Classmates Goes Viral," *The Epoch Times*, February 23, 2023, https://www.theepochtimes.com/teacher-on-leave-after-video-of-white-students-bowing-to-black-classmates-goes-viral_5086326.html.

a white student begins feeding them snacks while another white student fans them in the background.

The camera then shifts to the front of the seats, where several white students have gathered around, with one on her knees. *All the white students begin bowing with their arms outstretched toward the black students*." (Emphasis added)

The video, titled "Black History Month: The Shortest Month of the Year," gained 1.7 million views with mixed reviews. And the teacher was not fired. It took another viral stunt, the teacher grabbing books of all varieties from *Harry Potter* and *Holes* to a literal dictionary, as a protest of the State of Florida's stance against sexually explicit content. If the kids cannot read the doctrine of the Left's faith, they will not read at all. The kids would have continued to bow to the Left if their parents had not intervened.

If this doesn't sound like a cult hell-bent on getting your kids to drink the Kool-Aid, I do not know what to tell you, friends. The Left is going after your kids. Its members are pulling from the same book the Soviets and Nazis used because they are a religion-like cult dedicated to removing God and replacing Him with themselves. The school board is run by the state, which is run by elites, which are the priesthood to the gods themselves, because they are themselves the gods.

If you think this is merely me being dramatic, think back to the Aztecs or any other famous cult. After they try to make *you* sacrifice your kids, what do they usually do with them? *They* sacrifice them.

In Virginia, the secret side of this conflict started to emerge into the public's scope when a fifteen-year-old girl was coerced into having an abortion without her parents being allowed to know.[74] This girl, who under Virginia law is still a minor and must have parental involvement in medical decisions, was told by the staff at Bristol Women's Health Facility that she needed an abortion and could not tell her parents about it. The infant in the womb was this girl's child, and her parent's grandchild. But the experts killed it and pretended it was an accident until the young girl spoke up. The parents are now suing the organization for damages on behalf of their traumatized daughter and deceased grandchild. It is a tragedy. But the Left does not care.

Leftists would rather not report on the matter and continue showing their political adversaries doing something stupid than acknowledge what people are doing behind the scenes in our own communities. But more recently, as parents and families are beginning to take a larger interest in these stories, they're realizing that their kids are the targets of these attacks.

In 2021 and 2022, a national story covered Loudon County High School and its mishandling of a sexual assault on its property, and decisive actions to shut the father of the victim up. This concerned and passionate father had had the audacity to demand answers from the faculty and staff who covered up the assault, and he was rightly furious that his daughter was sexually assaulted by a man in a skirt and that the school covered it up to not anger the

---

[74] Micaiah Bilger, "Parents Sue Abortion Biz That Did Secret Abortion on Their Daughter," LifeNews.com, February 18, 2023, https://www.lifenews.com/2023/02/18/parents-sue-abortion-biz-that-did-secret-abortion-on-their-daughter/.

Left.[75] The case spurred a growing concern of parents who are sick of these violations of their rights and the targeting of their children. Slowly, over the past few years, the issue of kids getting involved in the culture war has brought millions of parents into the fray as the Left has begun to openly engage with those who dissent.

The Battle for the Public Square

Climate change has always been an avenue through which the Left has been able to fight publicly. After all, who wants to see dead fish in their rivers or animals dying for no reason? One of the first commands that God gave Adam was to tend to the Garden of Eden. But today, some on the Left have taken it a step further by acknowledging they are openly a religious organization.

The University of Helsinki openly confirmed it this year when it decided to give an honorary doctorate of theology to Greta Thunburg, of all people[76] You read it right. Miss "How dare you?!" is now going to be Dr. After the Left has gone out and taken over the traditional positions the church held in our society, such as education, poverty care, medical practices, familial responsibil-

---

[75] Steve Warren, "VA Judge Finds Transgender Teen Guilty of Sexual Assault in Loudoun County High School Girl's Bathroom Case," CBN, October 26, 2021, https://www1.cbn.com/cbnnews/us/2021/october/va-judge-finds-transgender-teen-guilty-of-sexual-assault-in-loudoun-county-high-school-girls-bathroom-case.

[76] David Strom, "University of Helsinki gives Greta Thunberg a Doctorate of Theology," HotAir, March 20, 2023, https://hotair.com/david-strom/2023/03/20/university-of-helsinki-gives-greta-thunberg-a-doctorate-of-theology-n538197?utm_source=substack&utm_medium=email.

ity, and so on, its members have now decided to make it official with their newest prophetess. She has already prophesied that the world will end (and been wrong every time) so they may as well let her replace the likes of John Newton, John Wesley, or Thomas Acquinas in favor of a more politically correct alternative who is too young to break the current tenets of the faith.

Why does this matter? Because it places her on equal academic footing with someone who attended a legitimate seminary for years in order to teach the truth. Like the teachers mentioned earlier, she is in a position of authority and her regime must come to pass or else the world will supposedly burn.

The Left is still lacking one thing since it became the "revolution" of the Sixties—legitimacy. Those on the Left need their people to win the popular vote for elections. They need everyone affirming them. Because as the Enlightenment dictates, the majority enables the ruling authority. But there is only one problem—they do not yet hold the majority.

Sure, there are Hollywood, Washington, D.C., and other major cities, but the speed at which their revolution (specifically this newest phase of the sexual revolution) has taken off does not mean that everyone is running right along with them. There is another worldview contesting them.

The City of God, in addition to those who acknowledge that there is a God, objective truth, or at the bare minimum realized that the Left is not God, oppose the revolt against nature.

In Berlin, when climate activists going by the dubious title, "the Last Generation," threw buckets of black paint on a series of glass panels showcasing the German constitution, the people were understandably upset.[77] These protestors literally threw paint over the free-speech clause of their constitution, who wouldn't be upset?

In August 2017, protestors defaced and vandalized the Peace Statue in Piedmont Square in Atlanta, Georgia.[78] The protestors claimed that they thought it was a racist statue (despite the clear imagery of the statue to the contrary), but refused to clean it up, stating their now-common mantra, "No Justice, No Peace." The statue was over 100 years old and commemorated the peace following the Civil War. Still, the message was clearly sent—until their version of history reigns supreme, there will be no peace. There will only be conflict.

Recently, we've seen this to be the case as Atlanta was once again under attack by domestic terrorists who are hunting, harassing, laying traps for, and shooting police and State Troopers attempting to uphold the peace of the community.[79]

If any other voices are heard besides their own, they will shut them up. There is no peace until one side wins. When Matt Walsh made a documentary on transgenderism, showing that "Transchildren are made, not born," the Leftists lost their minds.

[77] Timothy H.J. Nerozzi, "Climate Activists Deface Constitutional Monument in Germany with Black Paint, Posters," Fox News, March 4, 2023, https://www.foxnews.com/world/climate-activists-deface-constitutional-monument-germany-black-paint-posters.

[78] Chris Jose, Rikki Klaus, and Joe Bruno, "Peace Monument Vandalized During Anti-violence March Through Atlanta," WSB-TV, August 14, 2017, https://www.wsbtv.com/news/local/metro-shows-solidarity-after-violent-protests-erupt-in-charlottesville/590580616/.

[79] Rebekah Riess, Dakin Andone, and Nick Valencia, "23 Face Domestic Terrorism Charges After Arrests in 'Cop City' Protests at Planned Police Training Site in Atlanta," CNN, March 8, 2023, https://www.cnn.com/2023/03/06/us/atlanta-cop-city-protests.

Why? Because they are not tolerant. If you believe there is a God who makes people male or female exclusively, you must be made to shut up. The Left must have control of the public square because that is its most important temple. But not its *only* temple.

After the riot on January 6, 2021, on Capitol Hill, what did we hear most members of the House of Representatives call the Capitol building? A bastion of freedom? A symbol of solidarity? No. It was their "temple of democracy." Speaker Pelosi, after multiple Capitol Police officers lost their lives, gave a speech to honor those officers who died while in service of the People's House by stating, "Each day, when members enter the Capitol, this temple of democracy, we will remember his sacrifice…"[80] And we are back to the "sacrifice" and "temple" terminology of an explicit religion.

The cult is very defensive of its sacred spaces, and no one will be tolerated to speak heresy in its version of the public square or democracy.

The culture (pulling from the root word "cult") of the City of Man and the City of God cannot coexist. Cannot share the tabernacle. Cannot sit around the campfire and sing kumbaya, because the City of Man will not allow the City of God to champion objective truth. The City of Man does not believe any such thing exists.

These two cities are diametrically opposed.

If you voice disagreement with the current trend, there will be conflict—and we now see J.K. Rowling, Bill Maher, and Elon Musk counted among the conservatives. The window for what

---

[80] Brakkton Booker, "Lawmakers Honor Slain Capitol Police Officer Brian Sicknick in Rotunda," NPR, February 3, 2021, https://www.npr.org/sections/insurrection-at-the-capitol/2021/02/03/963598638/lawmakers-honor-slain-capitol-police-officer-brian-sicknick-in-rotunda.

counts as Left is becoming more and more strict as the Left tightens its doctrine and control.

Think about when the Left decries the nuclear family. Or when the Pew Research Center reports that monogamous male-female households are the most productive, healthy, and promising for children. The Left claims that the pollsters are being homo/trans/etcetera-phobic. Its members do not even consider the possibility that they might be wrong.

Why do we have a "Pride Month"? The same reason Christians have Advent, Epiphany, and Lent, and Jews have the Feast of Booths, Weeks, and Passover. It is a time of celebration and reflection as we look forward to the deliverance of those faithful to the true faith. For the former, it's total submission and adherence to the creeds of their personal feelings, and the latter is submission to Christ and loving the Lord with all your heart, mind, and soul, and loving your neighbor as yourself.

Happy *holidays*. Whether they are blocked off by month, week, or day, they are just that—holy days.

Our nation is in a state of conflict, but there is good news. We already know who wins.

Our Ways Are Different

Now the Lord is the Spirit, and where the Spirit of the Lord is, there is freedom. And we all, with unveiled face, beholding the glory of the Lord, are being transformed into the same image from one degree of glory to another. For this comes from the Lord who is the Spirit.... Therefore, having

> *this ministry by the mercy of God, we do not lose*
> *heart. But we have renounced disgraceful, under-*
> *handed ways. We refuse to practice cunning or to*
> *tamper with God's word, but by the open state-*
> *ment of the truth we would commend ourselves*
> *to everyone's conscience in the sight of God.*
> (2 Corinthians 3:17–4:2 ESV)

This chapter should bring into focus the clear divide between the Left's culture and ours. Now, there are some on both sides of the aisle who would love to selectively read verses from either canon and re-enact a Macabeean revolt, or go on a zealous and militant crusade for "the cause." There are plenty of commentators who will go on their platform and say, "We need to fight! Fight fire with fire!" and also "buy gold."

If you think you have to be the savior of your cause, you will fail tragically.

We must behave differently from the Left because our behavior in relation to each other and the world is different. It is much easier to sit on a street corner with a megaphone and tell people they are all going to hell unless they do what you say; after all, the Left does it all the time.

Christ died an innocent man, laying down His life for us. I saw a pastor the other day note that all sorts of people are willing to kill for Christ, but few are willing to die for Him. Likewise, we often want someone to fight a fight with us, and champion people who do anything but show the love of Christ to others. There are those on both sides who are ready and willing to call for protests if someone on their side gets arrested, or does not get his way, but the moment the other side begins fighting fire with fire everything escalates.

I think about this in relation to our fight in politics. Christians are not supposed to operate in an underhanded way. We're not supposed to selectively edit God's word and take Him out of context to advance our aims. Christians are explicitly called to avoid lying, deceiving, or bending the truth. Augustine took this thinking to the extreme and quit his job as a professor of rhetoric (essentially a modern legal professorship) after his conversion to keep himself from wanting to be hyperbolic.

On the radio, sometimes members of my audience get annoyed when I play longer full-audio clips instead of snippets tailored to make those I disagree with sound awful. I want to put the words, even of those I oppose, in proper context. I don't want to play *gotcha*. We can see things differently. We can interpret events differently based on our worldviews. But we are not supposed to be deceitful, conniving, and cunning. I do my best to, as fairly as I can, explain what my political opponents see as truthful. The better my listeners and I can understand their point of view, the better we can respond with the truth and our opinions to counter their positions, and hopefully win them over to our side diplomatically.

Much too often these days, Christians in politics behave no differently from everyone else. Some claim to be Christians to get the votes despite living terribly sinful lives and claiming they, "have nothing to repent," because they, "have a great relationship with God."[81] Some claim that "Satan is controlling the church,

---

[81] "Trump Has a 'Great Relationship' with God," CNN, video, https://www.youtube.com/watch?v=mFruUe4CEQ0.

the church is not doing its job," when the person in question is in the middle of divorce over his own numerous affairs.[82] But either way, if you do not vote for these people, or try to push an alternative with better morals or genuine faith, then you better be ready to shut up; because these people fight the same way the Left does and you will be made to care what they say when bearing the name of your Lord and Savior.

We have removed ourselves from the sovereignty of God and think we must act or else all will fail. But this removal simply shackles us and binds us to the world. Where the Spirit of the Lord is, there is freedom.[83] We can be truthful. We don't need to twist words, take people out of context, and play the games that others do.

It is bad for our soul and it is bad for our witness. We're supposed to draw the world to Christ. Reflecting the world does not do that. We offer a gospel of self, not of Christ.

In the real world, just this past year, my friends in the Southern Baptist Convention were at it again. When picking a new president, they played the ruthless game of American politics within the church. There was opposition research, out-of-context tweets, willful efforts to not understand people speaking plainly, and character assassinations of those involved masquerading as journalism. These Baptists think that they will pick their next president without the Holy Spirit. It is dreadful to watch the world creep into the church.

---

[82] Aila Slisco, "Marjorie Taylor Greene Clarifies How 'Satan Is Controlling' Catholic Church," *Newsweek*, April 27, 2020, https://www.newsweek.com/marjorie-taylor-greene-clarifies-how-satan-controlling-catholic-church-1701596

[83] 1 Corinthians 3:17, ESV.

But it is not just the Baptists who are having these internal conflicts, as most mainstream denominations battle with the reparations movement, sexual revolution 2.0, Black Lives Matter movement, critical race theory, and on and on—let alone issues, such as which gender God identifies as, changing the lyrics of classic hymns to be more progressive, and whether people struggling or openly engaging in homosexuality should be allowed, and even encouraged, to preach from the pulpit.

Christians, we can't be like the world, or we won't reflect Christ. It is hard. The temptation to tribalism pulls at all of us. But we are not a tribe. We are the church of Jesus Christ, and we must put our trust in Him, not our own efforts. We must "contend for the faith that was once for all delivered to the saints." (Jude 3b, ESV).

Above all else, we must show each other grace. We must allow each other to speak into the world and culture in Spirit and in truth without condemnation for doing a gospel-centered task in a way we might not.

Christianity requires us to not mount a heckler's veto over others in the church and resist sending the tribal mob off to enforce matters where in Christian liberty we must allow each other to act. Not everything you dislike is disliked by God, and God will not find fault in everything simply because you find fault in it.

Our ways are not the world's ways. I am convinced that social media in general (and Twitter/X specifically) is harming our ability to show each other grace and understand the necessity of liberty in the actions of Christian conscience that do not directly touch the orthodoxy of the church. We need the ways of Mary and of Martha, the differing views and passions of the various Apostles.

We need Jesus above all else. If we do not conduct ourselves differently, the world will associate us with the Left, and we will be indistinguishable from the cult that burns its heretics.

Unless the church acts like the church and contends for the faith of Love, Joy, Peace, Patience, Kindness, Goodness, Faithfulness, Gentleness, and Self Control, the world has already won. The quieter the voices of the true faith become in a world of Gnosticism and explicit secularism, the louder the voices contending for cultural civil war will become, and conflict will quickly turn to violence.

It is imperative that we remember, "the Lord is the Spirit, and where the Spirit of the Lord is, there is freedom."

CHAPTER 5

THE COMING VIOLENT STORM

Violence is the last refuge of the incompetent.
—Isaac Asimov

In 1789 at the beginning of the French Revolution, the crowd stormed the Bastille and freed the prisoners inside. The poor and middle class in France were fed up with the monarchy, nobility, and clergy. Years of wars had led to increasingly burdensome taxes, and like among the colonists in the U.S., there was a growing dissatisfaction among the people over their limited role in the political and social system.

After the storming of the Bastille, the French National Constituent Assembly issued the "Declaration of the Rights of Man and of the Citizen" which set out the basic human rights of liberty, equality, property, and the right to resist oppression. The common people of France overthrew the *ancien régime* (old order) of France. They rejected the monarchy's supposed divine right to rule and seized the land held by the wealthy Catholic

Church leaders. Many of the rich clergy, aristocracy, and nobility fled France, but not all escaped in time.

A young French lawyer, Maximilien Robespierre, rose to power during the French Revolution. He was known for championing the cause of the poor and destitute. He wanted the lower classes to have more political and economic power. When King Louis XVI balked at compromising with the new government, Robespierre broke with his historic stance against the death penalty and demanded the king's execution. Louis and his wife, Marie-Antoinette, were famously found guilty of treason and beheaded.

Robespierre and his comrades implemented a number of reforms that would later be hallmarks of socialist movements, like those in Russia and Italy in the early 1900s. Among these changes were government control of prices, increased taxation of the wealthy, free education for citizens, and welfare assistance for the poor. The new government also confiscated the land and property held by the nobility and clergy who had previously fled.

Wealthy clergy and rich churches had been targets since the beginning of the French Revolution for their association with the unfair taxation of the common people. But as the revolution became more violent, the revolutionaries sought to free themselves from all Christian influence. They stripped churches of religious statues, crosses, and bells. Clergy were forced to resign, and some churches were converted to temples dedicated to the worship of "Reason."

The calendar was also changed to remove any reference to Christianity. *Dimanche*, the French word for Sunday, was banned because it means "the Lord's day." Revolutionaries changed or banned religious holidays, saints' days, and all other connections to Christianity. Even the famous cathedral of Notre Dame in Paris was desecrated. The altar was replaced with an altar to liberty, the crucifix was replaced with the bathtub of the martyred revolutionary Marat, and young women danced around a woman dressed as the goddess of reason.

The French Revolution progressively grew more violent. From September 1793 to July 1794, more than 300,000 people were arrested. More than 40,000 died. Many without even the pretense of a trial. What were their crimes? Opposing the revolution or disagreeing with the revolutionary leaders was enough to be marked an enemy of the people. Anything less than full-throated agreement with the revolutionaries was seen as treason. The punishment? A trip to the guillotine.

Robespierre's influence in the revolution continued to grow as his old allies and future enemies found themselves alone before the mob. Eventually, there was nearly no one left to stand up to him. By this point the people had lost their grip on reality and built a paper mache mountain, where the Eiffel Tower now resides in Paris, to celebrate the triumph of Reason. Robespierre himself climbed the mountain and returned with paper mache tablets with their own version of the ten commandments on them, signifying their improvement of the old Christian ways.

But not everyone was pleased with Robespierre and his dictatorial leadership. The Reign of Terror ended when Robespierre was overthrown. He was executed by guillotine, just like so many before him. As the Scriptures teach, those who live by the sword will die by the sword. Revolutions devour their own. After the fall of Robespierre, a young colonel, Napoleon Bonaparte, rose through the ranks to lead France. Under Napoleon, France moved from a republic back to a monarchy. The more things change, the more they stay the same.

Cultural Suicide: America Without Christianity

It would be easy to read about the violence of the French Revolution and think that it could never happen here. After all, the American Revolution wasn't so destructive. And it's true that the American Revolution took a widely differing path with a very different outcome. The main difference between the two was Christianity. Of course, not all Founding Fathers were Christians. But the deists and agnostics among the American revolutionaries accepted the role of faith and Christianity in American society. As historian Mark Noll explains:

> In America, the aspirations of democratic liberty
> and the principles of Christian faith made peace
> with each other. In France, aspirations that were
> only slightly more radical and principles that
> were only slightly more traditional made war....
> In France, republicanism has been the partner of
> atheism. In America, republicanism has been the
> handmaiden of faith.[84]

---

[84] Mark Noll, "A Tale of Two Countries: The French and American Revolutions Followed the Same Philosophy—Except When It Came to Religion," *Christianity Today*, July 14, 1989, https://www.christianitytoday.com/ct/1989/july-14/tale-of-two-countries-french-and-american-revolutions.html.

Christianity provided a stable foundation for American society. The Founding Fathers enshrined religious tolerance and rejected a state religion in the Constitution and Bill of Rights. The danger of the new Gnosticism of the Left is that it creates chaos and fosters cultural instability. Without a shared foundation of truth and an understanding of right and wrong, we're at risk of becoming unmoored as a society.

Like the French Revolution, our culture is rejecting Christianity and embracing violence. When we are no longer joined by a common foundation as a nation, it's far easier for us to see each other as enemies than as fellow citizens with different ideas on how to advance our country.

If the religion of the Left is allowed to run its course, it will destroy our civilization. From ancient times, two-parent households have been considered one of the most stabilizing factors in society. Evidence overwhelmingly shows that the best way to break the cycle of poverty in this country is to graduate from high school, get married first, *then* have kids, and stay married. But our "tolerant" culture regularly attacks and mocks families consisting of a heterosexual married couple and their children. Why? Because traditional families and traditional family values contradict "LGBTQIA+" families and their values.

In the name of equality or equity, the Leftist religion declares traditional two-parent households privileged and unfair. Instead of supporting stable families and helping those in poverty achieve prosperity and security through stable families, the Left punishes and systematically dismantles traditional families. Inevitably it is wealthy, privileged Leftists who undermine two-parent households, leaving the poor to deal with the fallout. Sadly, the poor can't afford the economic and social consequences of a single-parent home, but a rich person with a trust fund can.

This is just one example of how the new Gnosticism is working to destroy our civilization. We're told that to sustain and protect the environment, which must be done at all costs, families must have fewer children to reduce their impact on the environment. Abortion is necessary to help control the population, for the good of society. No wonder the Left favors LGBTQIA+ "families." Their members can't procreate naturally. Abortion, same-sex relationships, transgenderism, environmentalism, even racial conflicts, all serve the end of population control.

Yet, by telling people that two-parent households are bad, incentivizing divorce, and decreasing population growth, the Left will not be able to sustain its welfare state. We're going to end up with a bunch of senior citizens and children born in poverty all dependent on the government. Unless there are enough young people propping up the social safety net through their taxes, the whole system will collapse. We're seeing it unfold right now in Europe where countries with low birth rates are struggling to support aging populations.

Violence: Converting by the Sword

For a long time, the Left has preached tolerance as a central tenet of liberalism. That has morphed into toleration of everything except intolerance, where intolerance inevitably is something that violates the Leftist belief system. When you refuse to tolerate what you define as intolerance, then you have the right to silence and punish those you deem intolerant. To achieve its utopia, the Left cannot tolerate dissent. Society must conform to its views. Those unwilling to conform will be forcibly converted or silenced.

The problem is that the Left, like Robespierre, is losing control of its own revolution. The revolution is starting to devour its own. No one is safe. Every week, there's some perfectly woke person who's no longer woke enough.

Consider J.K. Rowling. Rowling was wildly successful and popular, especially with millennials who grew up reading her Harry Potter series. She was considered a progressive, feminist icon. But like many feminists, she has found herself on the wrong side of the transgender divide. The feminists are split over how to incorporate men (claiming to be women) in the feminist movement.

Some are trans-inclusive and fight for transgender women to have the same access and privileges of all women. For example, they champion biological men who call themselves transgender women and compete in sports against biological women. Other feminists disagree on this point. While they are just as likely to support transgender "women" and protect them from discrimination and violence, they believe that it's unfair to biological women to compete against biological men. They prioritize protecting and advancing the feminist cause of women who are biologically female.

Trans-inclusive feminists disparagingly refer to these other feminists as TERFs (trans-exclusionary radical feminists). J.K. Rowling has publicly stated that both transgender men and women have been mistreated and need to be protected. But because she has also written about the erosion of women's rights and protections due to the demands of the transgender community, she is called a TERF and considered an enemy. She has come under heavy fire by Leftists who have called for boycotting her books and the games based on her series. And, Rowling had, indeed, been "canceled" in woke circles.

Given the attacks on someone as powerful and well-known as J.K. Rowling, it's not surprising that the Left has a perception of power. It certainly has clout within corporate America to steer money to its organizations, advance its causes, and indoctrinate others. The Left is feeding on the fumes of its perceived cultural clout which comes from the perception that it is dominant—but, is it really?

There is a silent majority of people who are increasingly frustrated with what's going on. Parents whose daughters are forced to compete against boys are concerned and angry. In corporate America with constant "diversity, equity, and inclusion" (DEI) training, people are increasingly agitated.

While it hasn't caught up yet, there is a growing cultural backlash against the Left's agenda. And that's one reason why there's such a push right now on the Left, particularly about the transgender community, to control the public narrative. Leftists fear that the tide is turning against them, and their only recourse is to silence dissent and create chaos and intimidation so that people feel alienated, isolated, and alone. They want the silent majority to think that they are outnumbered and give up the fight.

What the Left is promoting conflicts with reality. Men don't get pregnant. Women aren't dads. Women exist. Abortion is murder. As people push back against the societal upheaval, the Left is realizing that the path forward is coercion and force. The result is a growing level of violence in society. It's escalating. And, like a wildfire, it's going to run out of kindling. But how many people will be burned in the fire before it dies out?

Violent Revolutions of the 20th Century

The violence we're seeing may seem like a recent development, but historically violence has always been a part of Leftwing activism. In fact, violence has been part of the American story, and the world's story going back to Cain and Abel. But there's a pattern to violence and Leftwing movements that's obvious when you consider the last one hundred years.

The fascist, socialist, and communist movements spawned several violent revolutions during the past century. Each started with a utopian goal: to create a better or perfect society. The revolutions followed the same basic blueprint. Step one was to create an us-versus-them dynamic by finding someone to blame.

During the Russian Revolution, the revolutionaries blamed the Tsar and other nobility for the poor conditions of the Russian peasants. Mussolini blamed socialists for failing to support Italy during World War I. The Nazis blamed the Jews for the outrageous inflation and debt taken on since they conceded their loss in 1917. In Cuba, Fidel Castro blamed capitalism for exploiting the workers. Mao Zedong blamed the bourgeoisie and capitalism for undermining the efforts of the Communist Party in China to protect the proletariat.

Step two was removing these unwanted elements from society. These barriers were stopping the revolutionaries from achieving their utopian dreams. There were many ways to get rid of opposition. Propaganda and persuasion can work wonders in bringing people to your side. But ultimately each of these revolutions resorted to violence against dissent and any who stood in the way.

In Russia, the Tsar and his family were arrested and assassinated. The Bolsheviks silenced all political opposition. Their campaign of violence was known as the Red Terror and modeled itself after the French Revolution's Reign of Terror. As many as 200,000 people were executed between 1917 and 1922.

Benito Mussolini rose to power in Italy in the 1920s. He used fascist paramilitary squads known as the Blackshirts to stop dissent. The Blackshirts were known for their violent tactics. They killed the opposition and burned down their buildings. As prime minister, Mussolini was able to utilize the police to arrest and detain people who disagreed with him or worked against him.

The holocaust against the Jews in Nazi Germany began with antisemitic rhetoric and stripping Jewish citizens of their rights and property. Nazis enacted a pogrom of systematic violence against the Jews. For two days, mobs destroyed Jewish homes and businesses. They desecrated synagogues and stole artifacts and belongings. The destruction became known as *Kristallnacht*, or the night of broken glass. Many Jewish men were killed, and thousands were arrested and sent to concentration camps. The same concentration camps were responsible for millions of deaths.

In Cuba, Fidel Castro led a violent, military coup to overthrow the government. Afterwards, Castro ruled Cuba as an authoritarian dictator. Thousands of dissenters were executed, and thousands more imprisoned, intimidated, and deprived of their civil liberties.

During the Chinese Cultural Revolution, another Red Terror took place. Groups of revolutionary students known as the Red Guard sought to carry out Mao Zedong's vision for China. In his *Little Red Book*, Mao explained the need for violence:

> Every Communist must grasp the truth, "Political power grows out of the barrel of a gun." ...[85] Revolutionary war is an antitoxin which not only eliminates the enemy's poison but also purges us of our filth. Every just, revolutionary war is endowed with tremendous power and can transform many things or clear the way for their transformation.[86]

Red Guards purged China of Mao's enemies, destroying cultural and historical sites, such as museums and cemeteries. They confiscated property and sent people to be "re-educated." Millions were tortured, publicly humiliated, and killed.

In each of these revolutions, people's natural reluctance to violence had to be overcome. This was done by demonizing the opposition and ramping up fear and violent rhetoric. Violence became excusable behavior and even a necessary evil when committed for the good of society. Until dissent was quashed, there could be no peace. Until the unwanted elements of society were gone, how could there be utopia?

---

[85] "Political power grows out of the barrel of a gun." quote from Mao Zedong, "Problems of War and Strategy," (November 6, 1938), *Selected Words, Vol. II*, pg 224

[86] "On Protracted War," (May 1938), *Selected Works*, Vol. II, pg 131.

Anti-War Protests, Race Riots, and Eco-Terrorism

In the wake of the riots sparked by the death of George Floyd, journalist Nikole Hannah-Jones said, "Destroying property, which can be replaced, is not violence."[87] Her attempt to distinguish attacks against people from those on property falls flat when considering the historical connection between the two.

Terror tactics are designed to be psychologically violent. For example, the Ku Klux Klan was and remains a domestic terror organization. Though far less prevalent now, in its heyday, the Klan would engage in terror tactics to cause fear and flight among black Americans from the South. The Klan did not just lynch black people. Its members burned crosses in yards and burned down homes. A black family might go to church on Sunday and come home to a house in flames.

Just like the revolutions of the 20th century, people and their property have been regularly attacked and destroyed during the anti-war protests, race riots, and environmental activism starting in the 1960s. Jonah Goldberg summarized some of the most notable examples of the Left's violent history:

> These were the days when the militant Left wasn't dedicated merely to blowing up binary gender categories with tweeted "truth bombs," but to blowing up buildings, and occasionally people, with real bombs. During the summer of 1970 alone, there were 20 bombings a week

---

[87] Jackie Salo, "New York Times Reporter Says Destroying Property Is 'Not Violence,'" *New York Post*, June 3, 2020, https://nypost.com/2020/06/03/ny-times-reporter-says-destroying-property-is-not-violence/.

in California. "It's a wonderful feeling to hit a pig," Mark Rudd of the Weather Underground mused. "It must be a really wonderful feeling to kill a pig or blow up a building." Jane Fonda held "F*** the Army" rallies and in 1972 let herself be used by the enemy as a propaganda tool, even posing behind the trigger of a North Vietnamese anti-aircraft gun. The Black Panthers—lionized even by many liberals—made Black Lives Matter seem like a debating society. And as bad as the BLM and Antifa riots of 2020 were—and they were very bad—they pale in comparison to many riots in our past.[88]

The Weather Underground, a group formed to protest the Vietnam War and demonstrate for civil rights, bombed the United States Capitol in 1971. In 1972, it bombed the Pentagon. In 1975, it bombed the State Department. The members also plotted the assassination of a California State Senator in 1978.[89]

In the past few decades, the Leftwing Earth Liberation Front (ELF) and Animal Liberation Front (ALF) have carried out numerous terrorist attacks in the United States. The groups have burned down research facilities, destroyed property, and engaged

---

[88] Jonah Goldberg, "Mugged by Fallacy," *The Dispatch*, November 17, 2021, https://thedispatch.com/newsletter/gfile/mugged-by-fallacy/.

[89] Federal Bureau of Investigation, "Weather Underground Bombings," https://www.fbi.gov/history/famous-cases/weather-underground-bombings.

in other violence.[90] According to a 2001 report sponsored by the U.S. Department of Energy, "Leftist extremists were responsible for three-fourths of the officially designated acts of terrorism in America in the 1980s."[91]

ELF and the Weather Underground were only two of the groups promoting and carrying out acts of violence in the 1960 and '70s. The Black Panthers were formed in 1966 after the assassination of Malcolm X to oppose police brutality against African Americans. Members were recognizable by their black berets and leather jackets worn as they patrolled the streets in cities across the country. The group had numerous shootouts with the police. Founder Huey Newton was convicted of manslaughter after killing a police officer. Even within the organization, violent conflicts led to torture and murder.[92]

Los Angeles has been the site of numerous violent race riots. In 1965, a series of riots broke out in the Watts neighborhood. Dozens died, thousands were injured, and millions of dollars' worth of damages were done.[93] During the summer of 1967,

---

[90] U.S. Department of Homeland Security, "Science and Technology: Bombing and Arson Attacks by Environmental and Animal Rights Extremists in the United States, 1995–2010," https://www.dhs.gov/publication/st-frg-overview-bombing-and-arson-attacks-environmental-and-animal-rights-extremists.

[91] Karl Seger, "Left-Wing Extremism: The Current Threat," Oak Ridge Institute for Science and Education, April 30, 2001, https://digital.library.unt.edu/ark:/67531/metadc724454/m1/3/.

[92] Clayborne Carson and David Malcolm Carson, "Black Panther Party," in Mari Jo Buhle et al., eds., *Encyclopedia of the American Left* (New York: Garland Publishing, 1990), https://digitalcommons.wku.edu/cgi/viewcontent.cgi?article=1814&context=stu_hon_theses.

[93] History.com, "Watts Rebellion," June 24, 2020, https://www.history.com/topics/1960s/watts-riots.

more than 150 riots took place in cities across the U.S. In Detroit, rioting lasted five days. Forty-three people died, thousands were arrested, and nearly a thousand buildings were looted, vandalized, and destroyed.[94]

Riots erupted in Los Angeles in 1992 after the acquittal of the police officers charged with beating Rodney King. Fifty people died, more than 2,000 were arrested, and more than 1,000 businesses were damaged in the looting and arson. The total property damages were more than $1 billion.[95]

Waves of protests and riots took place across the country after the death of George Floyd in 2020. Millions of people participated in the demonstrations. Nineteen people died, thousands of civilians and police officers were injured, tens of thousands were arrested, and the property damages are estimated at $2 billion.[96]

Anti-fascism groups (Antifa) have been active in the U.S. since the early 2000s. Antifa members violently disrupt Rightwing demonstrations and protests. Brian Levin, director of the Center for the Study of Hate and Extremism, explains, "There's this 'It's going down' mentality and this 'Hit them with your boots' mentality that goes back many decades."[97]

---

[94]   History.com, "1967 Detroit Riots," March 23, 2021, https://www.history.com/topics/1960s/1967-detroit-riots.

[95]   Anjuli Sastry Krbechek and Karen Grigsby Bates, "When LA Erupted in Anger: A Look Back at the Rodney King Riots," NPR, April 26, 2017, https://www.npr.org/2017/04/26/524744989/when-la-erupted-in-anger-a-look-back-at-the-rodney-king-riots.

[96]   Brian Flood, "NY Times Ignores 18 Deaths, Nearly $2 Billion in Damage When Bashing GOP Bills Targeting Rioters," Fox News, April 22, 2021, https://www.foxnews.com/media/ny-times-ignores-18-deaths-2-billion-damage-gop-bills.

[97]   Jessica Suerth, "What Is Antifa?" CNN, updated May 31, 2020, https://www.cnn.com/2017/08/14/us/what-is-antifa-trnd/index.html.

In Atlanta in January 2023, Antifa terrorists enacted a "night of rage" after an Antifa member was killed by police after shooting an officer. Antifa operatives were protesting the construction of a police training center and threatened contractors, churches, and anyone opposed to their efforts. Antifa groups started flooding into the area planting pipe bombs and other things, taking over the land to deny the police their training facility to prevent the development of the land. They fire-bombed a youth facility and corporate offices, vandalized homes and churches, disrupted church services, shot a police officer, and burned businesses and police vehicles.[98]

Many of the anti-war protests and civil rights marches were peaceful. And it's important to remember the history of non-violent protests in our country. We have the right to gather, march peacefully, and make our voices heard. The contrast between peaceful protests and violent ones is stark. It's easy for the mob mentality to push people into violence and rioting, and we need to be constantly on our guard against being incited to violence.

Dangerous Times: Cancel Culture and Violence

We live in increasingly dangerous times. One wrong word choice, one misunderstanding, or one accusation can lead the mob to your employer or even to your door. You can be ruined, and no apology can bring you back unless that apology involves capitulation. A society that prides itself on pluralism thrives with differences

---

[98] Steve Warren, "Atlanta Police Arrest 6 on Charges of Domestic Terrorism After Antifa 'Night of Rage,'" CBN, January 23, 2023, https://www1.cbn.com/cbnnews/us/2023/january/atlanta-police-arrest-6-on-charges-of-domestic-terrorism-after-antifa-night-of-rage.

of opinion. But, increasingly, some opinions that were legitimate yesterday, last week, or last year are now unacceptable.

While lecturing Americans on race, sexuality, anti-biology, and "equity," corporations, most media outlets, and the Left are willing to glad-hand and do business with a Communist nation that runs real concentration camps, forcibly sterilizes its citizens, and kills or jails anyone who speaks up. Disney, firing an actor for a holocaust reference, willfully did business in an area of China that runs actual concentration camps. The NBA that lectures America on black lives mattering makes a tidy sum by ignoring Hong Kong lives. Nike, which employs self-promoting demi-gods of wokeness and failed former football quarterbacks like Colin Kaepernick to lecture Americans on their sins, makes a pretty penny from China's sins.

The disparity in cancellations is going to boil over to violence. We are, frankly, getting our first early tastes. Not a day goes by that Trump supporters, conservatives, Christians, and others not of the Left are portrayed as bad, evil, wrong, and worthy only of silence.

The media, corporations, and the Left are in sync—an American Taliban that doesn't take a life, but certainly is willing to destroy a life and ruin a career for wrong speak, wrong thought, and wrong belief. The disproportionate power of the Left will result in further radicalization on the Right, and it absolutely will lead to escalating violence.

Those on the Left may think themselves more civil or more tolerant, but they aren't. Their cultural antagonism toward those they deem "intolerant" is going to end badly for all of us. The woke are waging jihad against every aspect of purported racism in American culture. As we saw in the revolutions of the past century, it's a small step from violent words to violent actions against those who must be silenced.

The Left is following the same revolutionary playbook, and it will lead to its members re-embracing violence. The Left is intent on achieving its version of utopia. Bolstered by the media and cultural and academic institutions, its members believe that they are the majority and portray themselves as the dominant voice in the United States. They accuse conservatives and Christians on the Right of standing in the way of progress. They view the Right as a threat to democracy.

The doomsayers and "priests" of the Left have convinced themselves that we have only a decade to stop the destruction of the planet. They truly believe we're headed toward the end of humanity as we know it, and that the planet is at a tipping point. Therefore, the United States must act immediately. But the United States will not act because of Republicans, Joe Manchin, and corporations.

We have a group of people who believe they are the majority. They believe their work to save the planet is being stymied by conservatives who are a threat to democracy and in danger of taking over. They also believe that if they lose their positions of power we are all going to die. Given all of that, what do you think they will do to maintain power and silence dissent?

Be Angry, But Don't Sin

The Left wants you to believe that the real threat to the country is domestic terrorism from the Right. In fact, most recent articles on domestic terrorism downplay Leftwing terror and spotlight Rightwing violence. It is, to be fair, a real thing. We should not dismiss it. January 6, 2021, though it has been revised repeatedly by Republicans to excuse it, was a violent attack on our country and government. Conservatives, including politicians, are calling for civil war. GOP Representative Marjorie Taylor Greene called for a "national divorce," saying:

> We need a national divorce.
>
> We need to separate by red states and blue states and shrink the federal government. Everyone I talk to says this.
>
> From the sick and disgusting woke culture issues shoved down our throats to the Democrat's [sic] traitorous America Last policies, we are done.[99]

There really is part of the conservative movement that has decided to close off its mind. Its adherents have decided that we should not engage with people who disagree with us. They have decided that we should not listen to people who disagree with us. That is exactly what the Left does. Have we given up on persuasion and winning people over with our ideas?

I am noticing a trend of people of faith who are starting to behave like those who have no faith. In particular, I am noticing people of faith showing hostility and contempt for others in the

---

[99] Marjorie Taylor Greene, @mtgreenee, "We need a national divorce," X, February 20, 2023, 8:43 a.m., https://twitter.com/mtgreenee/status/1627665203398688768.

same way those others show. Many argue that it is time to behave just like them.

There's a temptation and a real danger to mirror what the other side is doing. The Left, cancel culture, and the rise in graceless contempt for others is part of spiritual warfare. And it is the dark side of the fight. So many on the Right are so focused on the darkness and evil spreading on the Left that they risk being surrounded by it on the Right. The darkness is spreading, not just on the Left but across the political and apolitical classes of American society. Paganism is rearing its head. It is moving quickly to infect, infest, and entrench itself into our lives. We have to be able to call it out on all sides and must resist the tribalism of the present age.

We are seeing the rise of a post-Christian Right that wants to just beat the Left. It holds the Left in contempt just as the Left holds the Right in contempt. It is bitter, humorless, and focused on fighting. It has as little grace as the Left. It is filled with self-proclaimed Christians who neither darken the doorway of a church nor crack open a Bible and even a few regular church attendees who've put political victory ahead of the cross.

Both sides are playing the devil's game. The devil cannot stand to be mocked. Neither can the people who think Jesus will save them from COVID-19 but have to take a cavalcade of pills to save them from heart disease, diabetes, asthma, and all the other ailments they have. The devil cannot stand to be mocked. Neither can the people who still believe that the election was stolen by electronic voting machines. The devil cannot stand to be mocked. Neither can the woke Left.

If we are acting and behaving, performing exactly as they are, we're no better than them. We're supposed to be salt and light.

We're supposed to provide a compelling contrast and not be exactly as they are just with different ideas.

I have for a long time cautioned people that the other side are your political opponents, not your enemies. We cannot respond to the coming violence from the Left with violence from the Right. Two wrongs do not make a right, nor does might make right.

Let me remind you of something that may be hard to grasp in the midst of the chaos swirling around us. They win. We lose. At least, from a worldly perspective, they're going to win way more often than us.

The pagans are going to do far better than most of us, or appear to. The people who leave God behind are going to shine on the big stage. Of course, the big stage is going to burn with them on it, so you need an eternal perspective. The Psalms are filled with laments over how the wicked prosper. They are well fed. They seem to have few troubles. They are prideful and can be violent. They are boastful, and people love them and love their behavior.

This is the portrait of the wicked, and they transcend politics and partisanship. They are in celebrity cultures of the Left and Right. Some are in the church, and some are even in the pulpit. They lack humility and possess a prideful certainty. They seemed to be so put together, so sharp, so brazen, and so popular with their crowd.

There is a tempting cry in politics these days from both sides that each side should behave as they perceive the other—ruthless, brazen, unethical, and out to win for the sake of winning. It is easy to get pulled into that mindset and try to separate your faith on

Sunday from your behavior the rest of the week. But that's impossible. Christ trumps all, including politics.

You must understand that the prideful, godless people are going to be popular and successful. You must also understand this—it is an act of God's mercy. While the world is literally the worst that believers will ever have, for those who reject God it is the best that they will ever have. When your political opponents are violent and do their worst to you, do not return evil for evil.

Love Your Enemies

> *Love your enemies, do good to those*
> *who hate you, bless those who curse*
> *you, pray for those who abuse you.*
> —Luke 6:27–28 ESV

You're going to want to despair. But you cannot despair. The Bible is filled with people reaching out to God in despair. They find comfort when God reminds them that He is still in charge. The sovereignty of God matters. It's going to get worse before it gets better.

The time is coming quickly that Christians in America won't feel comfortable in either party. Prominent evangelicals are now dogmatically insistent that no Christian can vote Democrat because of the party's fealty to the abortion industry, let alone the transgender lobby. I don't necessarily disagree. Ironically, Republicans have not cut federal funding for abortion. So, your choices are voting for those who support abortion, or those who oppose it, but continue to fund it.

Here is the truth. Neither party really likes you as a person of faith. One caters to you as a useful block of votes. But please don't pay attention to that same party that regularly and reliably has been funding Planned Parenthood for decades. You are useful as a vote, nothing more. Politics can't save you. But God can.

To God, you are His agent to advance His kingdom on this planet. Your job is to glorify Him, not a political party. The solution, my friends, is to remember to love your neighbors. You may want to hate them, but you have to love them. You have to be their neighbor.

You've got to be the guy who loves his neighbors so much that even your gay, trans-rights activist, tree-worshiping neighbor trusts you with his or her house key. If that person lives next door to you, he or she would know that if something happens, you'd take care of his or her house. I encourage you to continue to engage in politics. Be a light. Be a witness. Be a voice for the voiceless and a champion for righteousness and justice. But don't be disappointed when you fail, because you will fail.

When we stand before God on the Day of Judgment, He is not going to ask us who we voted for but how we advanced His kingdom. Too many Christians are losing sight of this and are trying to advance politicians and political agendas instead. These Christians take to various politicians and political causes with the zeal of Torquemada overseeing the Inquisition.

Do not tie Christ to a party. Do not bear your cross in the name of a politician. Show grace. Love your neighbor. Engage in the town square and in politics. But be in both to glorify God, not to advance sinners and their agendas. Be willing to be at odds with those around you for the right reasons. Whether sharing the burden of cancer or the burden of the church or the burden of culture, God's got this. All things work for His glory. Be encouraged. Do not be afraid.

You worship a God who holds the universe in the palms of His hands. He sends bread from heaven and water from rocks and raised you up from the dust of the Earth and stitched you together in your mother's womb. This world ends. He does not and you do not. That matters most. God first. Everything else second.

CHAPTER 6

THE VIRUS SPREADS

For certain people have crept in unnoticed who long ago were designated for this condemnation, ungodly people, who pervert the grace of our God into sensuality and deny our only Master and Lord, Jesus Christ.
—Jude 3–5 ESV

The race ended in a tie. Down to the hundredth of a second. Both leading participants had identical times for their race.

One swimmer remembers, "I touched the wall and saw there was a five by my name indicating that I got fifth…I also looked up, and I saw the number five by Lia's name and so, in that moment, I realized we tied…"[100] Riley Gaines had been competing in swim

---

[100] Cameron Jenkins, "Swimmer Who Tied with Lia Thomas Says Female Athletes 'Not OK' with Trajectory of Women's Sports," *The Hill*, April 1, 2022, https://thehill.com/homenews/3256180-swimmer-who-tied-with-lia-thomas-says-women-athletes-not-ok-with-trajectory-of-womens-sports/.

events throughout college in the NCAA bracket. Despite not winning first place, Riley remembers the pride she felt in that moment when she realized that all those girls did what was "seemingly impossible" and beat the man swimming next to her. But the story did not end there.

When the participants came up to the podium to receive their trophies, a decision had to be made about who would get the trophy for fifth place. Since the margin between fifth place and sixth was fairly substantial, and Riley had tied with a *man* for fifth in a *women's* swim competition, you would think she would take the trophy home. But no. The trophy went to Lia (formally William) Thomas, leaving Riley with nothing to show for her efforts.

Any parents would be outraged if their daughter didn't receive a trophy that is rightly hers. Even more so if the person she tied with was a man a whopping six inches taller than her. But the story did not end there.

After losing the trophy which she was entitled to, Riley and the other girls were told they needed to share the locker room with Thomas—who, despite claiming womanhood, still has all of his original parts (to put it politely). Outraged at the thought of being expected to share the women's locker room, a private space where everyone already feels vulnerable, with a fully biological man, Riley began speaking out against the insane rules the NCAA was pushing on female athletes.

She spoke across the country on college campuses, on talk shows, to news outlets, even on my show where I had the pleasure of meeting her. But all of these speaking engagements are the last place she, a twenty-three-year-old woman just starting her life, wanted to be. She wanted to focus on dental school, not have a political spotlight on her. But today, so few are bold enough to admit that men pretending to be women are taking over women's sports under the name of inclusion and tolerance.

While Riley used her words to combat these radical ideas, others decided to respond with violence. At one of her speaking engagements, transgender activists, claiming they were only trying to shut her up and stop her supposedly violent words, held Riley hostage at San Francisco State University. They chased her down hallways screaming profanities and repeating their mantra, "Trans rights are human rights." The mob pursued Riley until campus police stayed with her in a computer room for hours as the mob got out of control. The situation continued to escalate until San Francisco Police were called in to disperse the crowd.

During her flight from the event, Riley was physically hurt and threatened by the activists for saying what she believed. "I was physically assaulted by one person. I was struck twice, both times hitting my shoulder with the second strike grazing my face," she said.[101] Ironically, the Turning Point USA spokesperson who was working the event said that there had been much civil debate on both sides of the discussion until the violence broke out. For some reason, these activists decided that it would be better to shout her down and shut her up instead of debating her.

The religion of the Left, lacking a stable foundation, spurs its adherents—like most cults and new religions in history have done—to attempt a violent takeover. But small skirmishes of violence will not be the end of the escalation. After all, religious wars

[101] Natasha Chen and Cheri Mossburg, "Riley Gaines, Outspoken Critic of Transgender Athletes, Says She Was Attacked During Event at SFSU," ABC7 News, April 7, 2023, https://abc7news.com/riley-gaines-attacked-san-francisco-state-assaulted-ambushed/13099865/.

are nothing new. And as any person of faith knows, no one can serve two masters. Likewise, no one can appease two masters or love two different gods, no matter how loudly they shout their opponents down.

The Contagion

There is a virus spreading across the country. At the University of Minnesota Medical School, the dean, a renowned doctor, administered an oath to the incoming class of 2026. The students pledged to "honor all Indigenous ways of healing that have been historically marginalized by Western medicine," and fight, "white supremacy, colonialism, [and] the gender binary." Shamanism is back. Real medicine is out.

As voices on the Right began to express concerns about drag queen story hour for kids, the Left responded with gusto, providing more drag queen events aimed at kids. The backlash against conservatives hit harder and faster than anyone predicted. The Right is struggling to mount an effective defense. Meanwhile, the Left scoffs at the claims of "grooming" children, yet more stories are coming out about drag queens with criminal charges for sexual predation.[102]

As the Right has raised concerns about transgenderism, the Left has rushed to alter teaching, delete science, and embrace pseudoscience. While some would eagerly point out that humans are of

---

[102] Sarah Weaver, "Pennsylvania Drag Queen Who Performed for Children Charged with 25 Counts of Child Pornography," Parents for Megan's Law, July 8, 2022, https://www.parentsformeganslaw.org/pennsylvania-drag-queen-who-performed-for-children-charged-with-25-counts-of-child-pornography/.

the Hominidae family of mammals—as ten-year-olds across the nation have been taught for decades—it is important to remember that none within the family can change his or her gender. After raising two kids, my wife and I can confirm that biology hasn't changed since I was a kid.

It is a settled bit of science. The pagans of the Left, however, now claim that Homo sapiens are either a new family of animals altogether or an exception within the Hominidae family of mammals. Somehow, the Left wants us to believe, we can do what none of our closest animal relatives can.[103] Humans can change gender in the name of Science and Reason, not because biology has changed, but because politics have.

If you point out basic science, you're deemed a bigot. Medical doctors, psychiatrists, philosophers, biologists, and more are silenced, bullied, and badgered out of the academy for daring to point out the madness. Some, like Jordan Peterson, have even been silenced online for daring to ask people, "remember when pride was a sin?"[104] Deviancy has become normal, and normalcy is now deviant. If you disagree, you are hateful, and hate is violence. Even popular celebrities like J.K. Rowling and Gina Carano are not immune to the pagan wrath seeking to silence them from speaking truth to lies.

[103] Simón(e) D Sun, "Stop Using Phony Science to Justify Transphobia," *Scientific American,* June 13, 2019, https://blogs.scientificamerican.com/voices/stop-using-phony-science-to-justify-transphobia/.

[104] Emily Lefroy, "Twitter Suspends Jordan Peterson for Tweet About Elliot Page's Trans 'Sin,'" *New York Post,* June 30, 2023, https://nypost.com/2022/06/30/twitter-suspends-jordan-peterson-for-elliot-page-sin-tweet/.

In Atlanta, near where I live, a massive William-Sonoma store closed and new owners converted it into what is now one of the Southeast's largest metaphysical magic crystal shops. I kid you not. You can get tourmaline to ease your mental illness or sunstone to attract wealth and ward off evil spirits. Even its hiring section at Salary.com appears in the metaphysical section.

Undoubtedly, many of those on the Left who embrace the magic crystals have "In this house we believe in science," signs in their yard. But, as we've seen, their belief in science only goes so far. They continue to openly rebel against the created order and pursue chaos as they reject the God who "is not a God of confusion but of peace" (1 Corinthians 14:33, ESV). In rejecting Him and His order, they will soon jettison peace to pursuit power. They shall be as gods.

Sadly, this virus is infecting more than the political Left.

The Darkness Does Not Just Fester Over There

This virus is spreading among those of the Right, too. We just try to avoid eye contact with it because it is not a comfortable concept to swallow. After all, we are supposed to be the good guys. The party that ended slavery. The party of Lincoln, Ike, Reagan, and more. The one fighting the continuing drug crisis. The party that defends the Second Amendment and backs the police. The party seeking to end abortion. How can we not be the good guys?

I assure you the darkness is not just on the Left. There are those in TV, podcasts, and Washington who would like nothing more than for you to believe that we are the good guys on every subject. After all, you trust them to tell the truth, which is why you watch them over their competition. But what about news of vigilantism, rogue militia groups, or a racist crime by the Right? Too often, these fair and balanced sources discredit such claims, citing necessity or blaming bad individuals or Antifa. Sometimes that's true but not always.

Although we rightly remind those who want to undermine our Second Amendment rights that "guns don't kill people; people kill people," we ironically fail to hold people on our side responsible when they do wicked things. I have been guilty of this and welcome accountability on my show and in my life to make sure I present the truth accurately and overcome my bias before I point out bias elsewhere. It is not easy to do. But before condemning others for the specks in their eyes, we need to be able to acknowledge the logs in our own eyes.

There are bad guys on our side, too.

In particular, there's a resurgence of racism and white supremacy on the Right. Ross Douthat predicted this in his incredible piece "In Defense of the Religious Right." In that article, he closed by emphasizing, "[S]ome kind of religious conservatism must be rebuilt, because without the pull of transcendence, the future of the Right promises to be tribal, cruel, and very dark indeed."[105] I recommend you read the whole article. His point is that if you hate the Christian Right, wait till you meet the post-Christian Right. I alluded to this in the previous chapter, but it needs to be unpacked further.

[105] Ross Douthat, "In Defense of the Religious Right," The *New York Times*, October 15, 2016, https://www.nytimes.com/2016/10/16/opinion/sunday/in-defense-of-the-religious-right.html.

The Left gave up and expelled Christians who disagreed with its dogma. It traded philosophy for force and diplomacy for malice. I can safely say there are very few devoted Leftists who claim to be Christians and actually practice their faith. I know Democrats who are incredible Christians. Some of them are talented evangelists, who make virtually every conversation about God without batting an eye. In many ways I am jealous of how open and generous they are with their love, grace, and ability to reflect Christ to others. But these people are becoming a minority rejected by the rest of the Left.

In reaction to the growing pagan Left, many on the Right are now responding with the same levels of wickedness they have been subject to. Rightwing media outlets have begun preaching a doctrine of conflict. They seek to fight fire with fire. They act the same way as the Left by going on highly partisan TV stations, podcasts, talk shows, or Twitter/X and saying that if we don't fight back, we will all be destroyed. Unfortunately, combatting an idea and fighting the people devoted to an idea are two very different things. Practicing our civic authority and participating in hunting a minority are not the same. Rest assured when they say they will *fight* they mean it.

These days it seems more and more are crawling out of the woodwork. We are meeting them, and they are pagans like the Left—suffering the same social virus dragging them into Gnosticism. They embrace the same intersectionality and identity politics of the Marxist, postmodern Left. They're more alt-Right than Right. They're on the Right without conservative conviction. They lack the desire to conserve anything and seek only to rewrite, revise, and destroy their opposition. They are struggling to define a new ideology without Christianity, and seek to rewrite Christ, just as the Left has done.

Instead of Christ being the emotional lover of the LGBTQ+ who accepts all, embraces all, and tolerates all; Christ is the wrathful, vengeful Old Testament God whose tribe is white, not Jewish, and will wipe out sinners to the tune of Wagner's "Ride of the Valkyries."

I have encountered this manifestation of the post-Christian Right's idol and its redefined "Christianity."

In Georgia, two black teens murdered a white high school senior who was with his girlfriend at a Dave & Busters. The parents of the murdered teen said they forgave the murderers. The murderers will face justice according to the law. The parents want the murderers to face justice. But the parents refused to hate, and instead forgave. They summoned the peace that transcends all understanding to exercise a strength that no pagan possesses to forgive those who did violence to their family. May God bless them for it.

But the post-Christian pagans on the Left and the Right were enraged. I saw a tweet that stated, "This kid's body isn't even cold yet, and the parents and girlfriend are already falling all over themselves to forgive the murderers and move on? No Righteous [sic] anger? What a pathetic, broken culture this is." Suffice it to say, I was shocked and could not help but reply, "I think it's the epitome of Christianity to forgive even someone who kills your loved one."[106]

---

[106] Erick Erickson, Twitter, October 10, 2022, https://twitter.com/EWErickson/status/1579667018651176960?lang=en.

No one should condemn grieving parents for their response and demand that they engage in only one way. Particularly not if what you want is to satisfy your own emotional reaction and not what Christ Himself commands his followers to do.

It is baffling that Christian parents should be attacked for showing forgiveness—a strength, not a weakness, that pagans do not possess. We're not even talking about theological forgiveness of God toward sinners. We're talking about Christian parents of a murdered son forgiving their son's killers and the post-Christian alt-Right attacking the parents. Why? Because they want vengeance. Like the revolutionaries they are, they would rather see someone hauled up to the gallows in the public square to appease the mob.

This is as demonic as drag queen story hour—a manifestation of evil in another form—an evil that seeks to provoke bloodlust and shames the meek who will inherit the Earth, shames the pure in heart who will see God, and shames the peacemakers who will be called children of God. It is the mindset of the zealot who straps a weapon to himself to shame and harm others because they disagree. The alt-Right wants to wield the same power of fear and violence the Left has.

If you think my response was mild and inoffensive, imagine my shock the next morning when I opened my phone. Behold what I provoked:

> There is a disease of the mind that afflicts white people like Erick Erickson that makes them think it would be honorable to wash the feet of the murderers of their children especially if they

are not white. It is beyond pathetic and deserves nothing but contempt and disgust.[107]

In John 13:2–5, we read:

> During supper, when the devil had already put it into the heart of Judas Iscariot, Simon's son, to betray him, Jesus, knowing that the Father had given all things into his hands, and that he had come from God and was going back to God, rose from supper. He laid aside his outer garments, and taking a towel, tied it around his waist. Then he poured water into a basin and began to wash the disciples' feet and to wipe them with the towel that was wrapped around him.

Jesus washed Judas's feet, knowing that Judas would betray Him and lead to His murder.

The reaction to my response is not much different than the attempts by theological progressives who claim Christ didn't really talk about homosexuality so gay marriage is okay. It's eerily similar to those who defended enslaving Africans, arresting Jews, and legalizing abortion.

This demonic gospel of the alt-Right is no different from those who say that Jesus would support transgenderism because he said you must be "transformed." Or better yet, claiming that since the translators were all white, heterosexual males, we must

[107] Pedro L. Gonzales, Twitter, October 12, 2022, https://twitter.com/Don-JBacon/status/1580697904435470337.

therefore use the Queen James Bible—which is a real thing, and holds real evil in it, so I would not recommend it.

As you can see, small twists, over time, become large heresies.

Many on the Right are so focused on the darkness and evil spreading on the Left that they risk being surrounded by it on the Right. If we are not vigilant, we will not only be conflicting with the new Gnosticism over there, but our friends, family, and political prospects will have already sold their souls to the alt-Right god of vengeance and violence. The darkness is spreading. It is not spreading just on the Left but across the political and apolitical classes of American society.

Be mindful of those who have already slipped in among our ranks seeking to preach a new gospel. Look at the actions of those running for public office. Are they sleeping around while commending the biblical family? Are they attacking godly people to make themselves seem more sanctimonious? Are they claiming the church is demonic while preaching Gnostic truths that only they can reveal?

Paganism is waking up and rearing its head. It is moving quickly to infect, infest, and entrench itself into our lives. We have to be able to call it out on all sides and must resist the tribalism of the present age.

Our Lord and Savior Jesus Christ was not betrayed by either the Sadducees or the Pharisees but by one of His hand-picked disciples. Do not hate the Left so much that you ignore what festers on the Right. The darkness is spreading. The only thing that can stop it is the light of the real Christ and the real gospel, not the Jesus remade in the image of the Left and alt-Right.

Rhetoric Leads to Violence

On June 8, 2022, Nicholas Roske traveled to the home of Brett Kavanaugh, an associate justice of the United States Supreme Court, with a plan. Before going through with his design, he called the District Police. The transcript of the call was chilling:

> Montgomery County, 9-1-1. Are you thinking of hurting anyone, including yourself?
>
> *Brett Kavanaugh, the Supreme Court Justice.*
>
> Do you have access to any weapons?
>
> *I brought a firearm with me. There is pepper spray. There is a knife.*
>
> Are you on foot?
>
> *I'm just standing in front of the house.*
>
> What, were you coming there just to hurt him?
>
> *Correct.*[108]

Exactly two weeks later, the justice did his job and ruled on the very case his assassination was intended to stop. In those two

---

[108] Jordan Fischer, "911 Audio," WUSA9, June 9, 2022, https://www.wusa9.com/article/news/crime/911-audio-california-man-told-dispatcher-he-needed-psychiatric-help-wanted-to-kill-justice-brett-kavanaugh-nicholas-john-roske/65-6503396e-cc49-4796-b7ac-2782f77641ad.

weeks, Republicans were in an uproar, Democrats were on the defensive. The ruling was made, and no one was killed. But the Left refused to reflect on what may have led this man to break into the justice's home, kill him, and then kill himself, as he testified had been his intent.

Roske thought Kavanagh was a threat to democracy and needed to be stopped. He was told that was the case, anyway. But when we look back, who was saying anything like that? Who was telling people that conservatives on the Court were going to destroy freedom as we know it? Who specially targeted Kavanagh as the dragon needing to be slain to save the millions of women who need to abort their children?

Crickets.

Justice Kavanagh's hearings before the House and Senate to be confirmed to the Court were a complete and utter demonization of the man. No matter what he said, did, proved, or who testified, the Democrats were adamant that he wanted to subjugate women and single-handedly send them back to the Dark Ages. His party alone defended him. The same party the president calls semi-fascist.[109] And the party that former House Speaker Nancy Pelosi calls enemies of the state.[110]

But the real threat to democracy, according to these same sources, are the seventy-four million people who voted for Donald

---

[109] "Biden Slams 'MAGA Republicans,' Compares Philosophy to Semi-Fascism," CBS News, August 26, 2022, https://www.cbsnews.com/news/biden-maga-republicans-semi-fascism/.

[110] Griffin Connoly, "'Enemies of the State': Pelosi Rips Trump and Republicans for Undermining Faith in 2020 Election Results and Mail-in Voting," *The Independent*, August 26, 2020, https://www.independent.co.uk/news/world/americas/us-politics/nancy-pelosi-trump-republicans-mail-in-voting-usps-louis-dejoy-2020-us-election-a9687706.html.

Trump, before the Capitol riot, and are therefore responsible for the assault on the Temple to Democracy. Instead of acknowledging that Americans can disagree on politics, they see their political opponents as the enemy.

Joe Biden and the Democrats offer us the idea that Donald Trump provoked riots and violence in the country with his words. The January 6 Committee's entire argument hung on the idea that Trump's foolishness with his words that day equated to leading the assault. If that is true, then shouldn't the Left calling the Republican Party a domestic terrorism front be equally dangerous?

MSNBC and CNN refer to anyone who ever agreed with Trump as racist, white nationalists, even though many of them are not white. Make America Great Again hats popularized by the former president were constantly blasted by the media as the new Klan hood. But, when Chuck Schumer says we need to hunt down justices, or representatives say that if you enter an elevator with a justice you need to make sure only one of you leaves alive, they are not responsible for the consequences.

A man attempted to kill Brett Kavanaugh. According to the Left, he was fired up by, among other things, Court decisions on guns and decisions on abortion. Joe Biden has never condemned it. Merrick Garland has never gone out and prosecuted the people protesting in front of Supreme Court justices' homes, though it is against federal law to do so. The FBI has declined to investigate the fire-bombings of pregnancy centers around the country, and its focused on alleged fascism from the Republican Party.

But the pendulum always swings.

Violence Begets Violence

In March 2021, a lone gunman arrived at multiple massage parlors in the metro Atlanta area. He killed eight women who worked there. When the jig was up, he called his wife to help him.[111] The police arrested him. He is awaiting charges on twenty-three accounts related to the crime. Capital punishment is on the table, and he has pleaded guilty to four of the murders. Justice will be served.

But if you remember the story breaking, you may remember how the media largely covered the massacre. I'm sure you remember six of the eight killed were of Asian descent. More likely you remember the narrative revolving around race-based hate crime. Usually, when people commit a violent crime against people of a specific race, they themselves acknowledge the people were targeted for that reason.

In this case, the gunman claimed he was a sex addict who started with pornography and worked his way up to visiting massage parlors he said were brothels. He further said he tried to break his addiction but only fell deeper into it, unable to escape. He testified he did what he did to find an escape. What he did was evil in every respect.

This is what happens when people fight fire with fire. Eight dead, one wounded, and another waiting to be executed. Whether or not the spas were a cover for brothels does not matter as much as what the coverage of the story reveals. There are those in our country who would rather point at this and say look what guns do,

---

[111] Derrick Bryson Taylor, Christine Hauser, "What to Know About the Atlanta Spa Shootings," *The New York Times,* updated July 27, 2021, https://www.nytimes.com/2021/03/17/us/atlanta-spa-shootings.html.

and others who would say these women got what they deserved. Both responses are terrible.

Violence needs to be condemned. Regardless of what side of the aisle it stems from, vigilantism is wrong because it forfeits people's constitutional right to a fair trial. The gunman will get the trial and consequences he deserves. His victims did not get that chance. But what's more, no one seems to care about his professed motivation as a self-identified sex addict.

In March 2023, a woman who identifies as a man, shot and killed three teachers and three students at an elementary school connected with Covenant College.[112] Obviously, when the media began reporting differing stories on a female or male murderer, people voiced their confusion as the story seemed purposefully vague. But when Republicans dared refer to the criminal as a woman—which she is whatever pronouns she uses—the media lost their minds.

"Gender activists," as they like to call themselves, immediately accused those who were confused or called the shooter a woman of "deadnaming" the woman who took the lives of innocent children and teachers.[113] A surprising number of people began defending the shooter and the decisions she made leading up to the massacre. The press secretary for the governor of

---

[112] Adeel Hassan and Emily Cochran, "What We Know About the Nashville Shooting," *The New York Times*, April 12, 2023, https://www.nytimes.com/article/nashville-school-shooting.html.

[113] Cameron Parkins and Logan Harding, "Cis School Shooters Aren't Identified by Their Gender. So Why Was the Covenant Shooter Called Out for Being Trans?" *Pride Source*, April 11, 2023, https://pridesource.com/article/cis-school-shooters-arent-identified-by-their-gender-so-why-was-the-covenant-shooter-called-out-for-being-trans/.

Arizona went so far as to tweet a meme depicting a woman holding up guns that read, "us when we see transphobes."[114]

Leftists are fools. It is exactly this kind of rhetoric that leads a mentally disturbed person to murder his or her neighbors because they disagree over politics. But the foolishness and manipulation does not stay on the Left, but is spreading on the Right, and those suffering from mental health crises are at risk of manipulation by these rhetorical attacks.

When the Left pushes a narrative that everyone on the Right is the devil incarnate, people on the Right do not take that well. In fact, they react.

On the show *InfoWars*, Kanye West (now going by "Ye") dawned a black ski mask and was accompanied by the known white supremacist and propagandist Nick Fuentes.[115] This imagery was already not great, but worsened when Kanye claimed that the Holocaust never happened, that he admires Hitler, and that he loved Jewish people but also Nazis. Kanye has bipolar disorder, has stopped taking his meds, and recently went through a rough divorce which he claims stemmed from his porn addiction. Fuentes is a known liar and has clung to Ye like a leech. According to Ye, Fuentes showed him that Jews are the ones responsible for creating and getting him hooked on porn.

---

[114] Zoë Richards, "Top Aide to Arizona Gov. Katie Hobbs Resigns Over 'Transphobes' Gun Tweet," NBC News, March 29, 2023, https://www.nbcnews.com/politics/politics-news/top-aide-arizona-gov-katie-hobbs-resigns-transphobes-gun-tweet-rcna77307.

[115] Nikki McCann Ramirez, and Ryan Bort, "Kanye to Alex Jones: 'I Like Hitler,'" *Rolling Stone,* December 1, 2022, https://www.rollingstone.com/politics/politics-news/kanye-west-alex-jones-i-like-hitler-1234639617.

Kanye West has traditionally been a trendsetter living on the fringe of cultural norms and extremes. Do you think it is an accident that a public figure with a history of mental illness would surround himself with people who have a dangerous and racist vendetta? It is not. They want disciples and will take advantage of the platform and the prestige that Kanye brings. Simultaneously taking advantage of Ye's loosening grip on reality.

Ye is lonely and losing his mind on his own, with evil people whispering in his ears. The man who arrived at Justice Kavanagh's home was a lonely man who believed the rhetoric of the Left and decided to "fight" like he was told. The Atlanta and Nashville shooters continue the escalating violence of people who lose hope in democratic discourse and opt to destroy what their cultural leaders call evil. They are zealots. They are lonely. They are looking for purpose and a place in this world, and what they find is content online dedicated to pushing them to the extreme.

The Isolation of the American Mind

A lack of community and lack of identity are growing problems in our culture. People struggle to know their purpose. They want to be a part of something bigger than themselves, but often do not even know who they are or what they want to do. Because they live online, they are accustomed to censoring, editing, and filtering who they are, and tailoring what others see.

Every single person needs some level of community, though some do not recognize it as much as others. Right now, our country is going through a tumultuous change as the religious vacuum is waiting to be filled, and the new Gnostics are clamoring to fill it with their different cults.

COVID-19 accelerated the isolation crisis as people stayed home and looked to technology to bridge the gap between themselves and others. As people became lonely and afraid, many found online communities that fed their fears and their hatred of others.

People want community.

Online is not the same as being with people face to face. People put silly backgrounds on Zoom. They can forget to brush their teeth. They don't have to put on pants. It's not real life. Studies are coming out showing how video calls, by showing everyone at all times, treat every individual in the meeting as if he were the speaker. The resulting constant eye contact is incredibly taxing for everyone.[116] Beyond taxing, having people constantly looking at you cheapens the importance your brain places on the attentive eye contact you receive while speaking. It leaves us emotionally exhausted as we work overtime to interpret body language and interact virtually.

You try to see each other, but it's just not the same. We all know it's just not the same for real, tactile communities where you can actually get a sense of the person. I've got friends who come over on Sunday nights, a very small group of people. I love it. When my wife and I invite people to come hang out with us at the house, we always keep it small because people engage more in small groups. It's easy to fade into the background when you're

---

[116] Vignesh Ramachandran, "Stanford Researchers Identify Four Causes for 'Zoom Fatigue' and Their Simple Fixes," Stanford News Service, February 23, 2021, https://news.stanford.edu/press-releases/2021/02/23/four-causes-zoom-fatigue-solutions/.

surrounded by people. But my gosh, you're with a handful of people? You have to be honest! They can see you squirm under tough questions. They will keep you humble and encourage you. They are gifts from God Himself.

If you isolate yourself from the people who care about you beyond your immediate family, you're going to be anxious. You're going to be more worried. You're going to be more fearful.

I love what I do. I'm so blessed to be able to sit behind a microphone and talk to people. I'm not an extrovert, so this set-up is ideal. It's me and a camera and my computer. I've got some text messages flowing in, and otherwise I don't have to be around people. It's fantastic. And I can shield myself. But I recognize my need for people in person, in my life. It's not good for us to be alone.

If you want to combat the violence and collapse of mental health in our country, be there, in person, for your family, friends, and community. Be wise about your words. If Jesus fought fire with fire, there would be seven billion people crucified across the globe. But He didn't. He showed mercy, grace, and love even to those who hated him. He enjoyed fellowship with his friends and whichever members of his family still talked to him. He condemned violence telling Peter that those who live by the sword die by the sword. We must also condemn violence and evil wherever it springs up.

You probably have someone in your life who could use some hope. Judging by how things are going at the time of this writing, another tragedy has probably just happened near someone you love. Call that person. Pick up your phone, call, and see if you could get together just to chat.

You will do yourself, and that person, a world of good. You're thinking of someone right now. Your mom, sibling, cousin, friend, acquaintance, co-worker, or someone who gave you his card and you've been meaning to get in touch. Maybe you haven't talked to in a while. You've been meaning to, and you feel guilty about it. Pick up your phone, call that person, see how she's doing, and try to reconnect. Then keep reading. The rest of the book will focus on how to find hope in the midst of the hopelessness around us.

CHAPTER 7

BE ANGRY, BUT DO NOT SIN

If you do what is right, will you not be
accepted? But if you do not do what is right,
sin is crouching at your door; it desires to
have you, but you must rule over it.
—Genesis 4:7 (NIV)

All around the country, the Left is punishing conservatives, bringing lawsuits, shutting down businesses, vilifying traditional Judeo-Christian beliefs, and demanding that people worship the new Gnostic idols of diversity and identity. Nothing less than complete approval and full-throated support of woke ideology is enough to satisfy the Left.

A dozen pregnancy centers across America have been torched. More have been vandalized. Many of the pregnancy centers are run by churches or Christian organizations. They provide pregnancy screenings for women, ultrasounds, neonatal pregnancy care, diapers, and more to support women during and after pregnancy. They do not, however, provide abortions, and many counsel against abortion.

They are, therefore, the enemy of the Left. These centers have been subject to harassment, protest, condemnation, and now fire-bombings.[117] A common pro-abortion talking point is that pro-lifers only care about stopping abortion, not supporting women and children. These centers care for and support mothers and babies before and after birth.

Meanwhile, a dozen pro-life activists have had their doors kicked in by the FBI in dawn raids. Those activists have been held at gunpoint, dragged from their homes in front of their families, and arrested for violating a federal law making it a crime to obstruct access to an abortion clinic.[118]

More than one of these people were previously investigated by authorities, and no charges were brought because they did not actually obstruct access. They just protested at the clinics. Conservatives are rightly angry to see the Justice Department ignore arson attacks on Christian-run facilities while seeing pro-life activists aggressively arrested for protesting peacefully.

Our children are facing attacks and inappropriate behavior by the same people on the Left who claim to care for them. Drag queen story hour has become common at libraries, schools, and even bars across the country. Men dressed up in garish make-up

[117] Joe Bukaras, "Pregnancy Clinic Firebombed in 'Jane's Revenge' Attack Sues Police for Surveillance Footage," Catholic New Agency, September 21, 2022, https://www.catholicnewsagency.com/news/252352/pregnancy-clinic-firebombed-janes-revenge-no-arrests.

[118] Jon Brown, "Lawyer for Pro-Life Activist Arrested by FBI Blasts 'Outrageous Abuse of Power' from DOJ: 'Pure Intimidation,'" Fox News, September 27, 2022, https://www.foxnews.com/us/lawyer-pro-life-activist-arrested-fbi-blasts-outrageous-abuse-power-doj-pure-intimidation.

and risqué outfits are reading stories to kids. Many of the books promote LGBTQIA+ themes like "Santa's Husband," "If You're a Drag Queen and You Know It," "The Hips on the Drag Queen Go Swish Swish Swish," and "And Tango Makes Three."[119] Who decided this was acceptable? Why should our children be subjected to this indoctrination?

Middle school students in Wisconsin are facing charges from their school district for sexual harassment. They are being investigated under Title IX, which bans gender-based harassment and name-calling in schools. Why? Because they didn't use their classmate's preferred pronouns "they" and "them."[120] Bullying and harassment are all too common in schools, and such behavior needs to be addressed. But using "he/she" instead of "they" isn't bullying or sexual harassment.

In northern California, a middle school helped an eleven-year-old girl undergo gender transition without her parents' knowledge or consent. After the girl told her school counselor that she "felt like a boy," the school began calling her by a boy's name, gave her information about binding her breasts, and connected her with local groups to support her through her transition. The school district's policy is to withhold information from parents about children interested in gender transition unless the

[119] Jaweed Kaleem, "How Drag Queen Story Hour Became a Battle Over Gender, Sexuality and Kids," *Los Angeles Times*, February 22, 2023, https://www.latimes.com/world-nation/story/2023-02-22/drag-queen-story-hour.

[120] Emily Matesic and Gray News staff, "Middle Schoolers Accused of Sexual Harassment for Not Using Preferred Pronouns, Parents Say," 14 News, updated May 15, 2022, https://www.14news.com/2022/05/16/middle-schoolers-accused-sexual-harassment-not-using-preferred-pronouns-parents-say/.

student consents in writing. The girl's parents are understandably upset with the school for denying their parental rights.[121]

Our children are also being indoctrinated through critical race theory. Students in public schools are being taught to believe in racial essentialism, systemic racism, and collective guilt. In California, third-graders had to do an exercise ranking themselves by the "privilege" they have by virtue of their race and ethnicity. In New York, kindergarteners were shown a video on police violence and racism, including images of dead black children. Arizona's education department provided materials on "equity" and racism to public schools. According to these resources, children under five may already be racist and biased in favor of "whiteness."[122]

Additionally, public schools around the country are encouraged to celebrate the Black Lives Matter (BLM) "Week of Action." The purpose of BLM in the schools is much more than simply addressing racism and promoting the value of black lives. The goal is to indoctrinate students with the radical guiding principles of BLM, including restorative justice, globalism, LGBTQIA+ affirmation, and "black villages." According to BLM, black villages are a commitment to "disrupting the Western-prescribed nuclear family structure requirement by supporting each other

[121] Aaron Kliegman, "California School District Accused of Secretly Counseling Child to Transition Gender Faces Parents' Wrath," Fox News, February 19, 2023, https://www.foxnews.com/politics/california-school-district-accused-secretly-counseling-child-transition-gender-parents-wrath.

[122] "Yes, Critical Race Theory Is Being Taught in Public Schools," *Washington Examiner*, July 12, 2021, https://www.washingtonexaminer.com/opinion/yes-critical-race-theory-is-being-taught-in-public-schools.

as extended families and 'villages' that collectively care for one another and especially 'our' children."[123]

The attacks are even more blatant in our colleges and universities. Like many universities, Portland State University holds an annual "sex week" which has included a workshop on how to care for BDSM leather products. Other events held during "sex week" include promoting the positive benefits of polygamy, mainstreaming LGBTQ+ sexuality, and belittling traditional views on sexuality ridiculed as the "cult of virginity."[124]

Ohio State University's "sex week" had a workshop called "Treat Yourself: Masturbation and Self-Exploration" and another called "Valentine's for Abortion Providers" where students would make thank you cards to send to abortion providers.[125]

Tulane University's 2023 "sex week" offered workshops on "Polyamory & Polyqueer Relationships" and a "Genital Diversity Gallery," which "showcases SEX-ED + models...anatomically exact tools, based on human molding techniques...[representing] the vast spectrum of human life (assigned-male, assigned-female, intersex, trans, and with voluntary or forced surgeries) to destigmatize genitals and celebrate the diversity of bodies that exist."[126]

[123] Black Live Matter at School, "13 Guiding Principles," https://www. blacklivesmatteratschool.com/13-guiding-principles.html.

[124] Joe Silverstein, "Portland State University's 'Sex Week' Touted 'Chicanx Sexuality,' Derided the 'Cult of Virginity,'" Fox News, March 7, 2023, https://www.foxnews.com/media/portland-state-universitys-sex-week-touted-chicanx-sexuality-derided-cult-virginity.

[125] Adam Sabes, "Ohio State University 'Sex Week' Event Encourages Students to 'Thank' Abortion Providers," Fox News, February 6, 2022, https://www.foxnews.com/us/ohio-state-university-sex-week-event-encourages-students-to-thank-abortion-providers.

[126] Tulane University Sex Week, "2023 Events," https://sexweek.tulane.edu/sex-week-2023-schedule/.

Religious liberty has been a hallmark of our country from its founding, but conservatives are being fired for their views. In New York, an account clerk was fired because he refused to attend mandatory training on LGBTQ+ identity and discrimination.[127] A tenured professor lost his position at Chicago's North Park University because his traditional views on marriage were "too extreme" for university administrators.[128]

Jessica Tapia, a teacher in Southern California, was fired after she refused to follow the school district's transgender policies. These policies included allowing biologically male students to use the girls' locker room and lying to parents about their children's gender transition.[129] Dr. Allen Josephson was demoted, ridiculed, and fired for saying that children should be treated for the psychological issues underlying their gender dysphoria instead of being given hormones and puberty-blocking drugs.[130]

[127] Kaelan Deese, "New York Employee Fired for Skipping LGBT Training on Religious Grounds Loses Appeal," *Washington Examiner*, March 15, 2023, https://www.washingtonexaminer.com/restoring-america/faith-freedom-self-reliance/new-york-employee-fired-skipping-lgbt-training-loses-appeal

[128] Carl R. Trueman, "The Cancellation of Dr. Nassif," *First Things*, September 1, 2022, https://www.firstthings.com/web-exclusives/2022/09/the-cancellation-of-dr-nassif.

[129] Shawn Akers, "Christian Teacher Fired for Refusing to Participate in 'Lies from the Devil,'" *Charisma*, February 22, 2023, https://charismamag.com/spiritled-living/christian-teacher-fired-for-refusing-to-participate-in-lies-from-the-devil/.

[130] Ryan Everson, "A University Effectively Fired this Professor After He Spoke at a Conservative Think Tank," Alliance Defending Freedom, November 18, 2019, https://centerforacademicfreedom.org/a-university-effectively-fired-this-professor-after-he-spoke-at-a-conservative-think-tank/.

And the list goes on. Story after story. Day after day. We have every reason to be angry about what's going on in our country. It's not just the deviancies of the Left that scream out for normalcy. The post-Christian Right defines itself by "owning the Left" and works to keep its own outrage machine going. Lots of people are caught in the middle, pulled by both sides, confused about where they belong.

As the culture has shifted rapidly to the Left, the temptation is to get even, get ahead, and "punch back ten times harder." This kind of escalation feeds the outrage, sells airtime, and wins votes, but it's self-defeating. As each side pushes the other to more radical extremes, the silent majority in the middle pays the price. It's not wrong to be angry, but we must be careful not to let our anger consume us and lead us to respond in ways we will all regret.

Retaliation Is Not the Answer

> *You have heard that it was said, "An eye for an eye and a tooth for a tooth." But I say to you, Do not resist the one who is evil. But if anyone slaps you on the right cheek, turn to him the other also. And if anyone would sue you and take your tunic, let him have your cloak as well.*
> —Matthew 5:38–40 (ESV)

In January 2022, protesters in Canada organized a series of convoys to rally at Parliament Hill in the capital city of Ottawa. The "Freedom Convoy" was formed to protest the COVID-19 vaccine requirements for truckers crossing into the U.S. Some protests blockaded border crossings and cities across Canada.

A Christian crowdfunding website, GiveSetGo, hosted a fundraiser for Canadian truckers involved in the convoy after GoFundMe announced it would not send funds raised for the convoy to the protesters. Hackers got into the GiveSetGo website and made personal information about the donors available to the news media. The media used the information to target and harass the donors. Some lost their jobs. Some had their bank accounts frozen. Some had their businesses threatened.

I expected someone would retaliate by outing the information of the reporters and the hackers who did this. But that expectation of retaliation came from the sin within me. The situation prompted a conversation with my friends about how Christians should respond when the world sins against us.

Consider the lesson of Cain and Abel. Cain killed his brother, Abel, out of jealousy. God accepted Abel's sacrifice, but not Cain's. People often struggle with that passage wondering why God liked Abel's offering more than Cain's. Some assume God preferred animal sacrifice instead of fruit and vegetables. But it wasn't about what kind of offering God wanted. It was about Cain's heart. Had Cain given the same sacrifice with a heart that truly loved God, the outcome would have been different. We see the evidence of Cain's hard heart in his violence toward his brother.

Cain wasn't angry about unrighteousness. He wasn't angry at someone else's sin. It was anger and jealousy toward his brother. And God warns Cain, telling him that sin was crouching at his door, ready to devour him. Instead of listening to God's warning and repenting of his attitude toward God and Abel, Cain let his anger lead his actions when he killed his brother.

The temptation is for us to direct our anger at people, our brothers and sisters made in God's image. We get mad at people because they're doing unjust or sinful things, and they appear to prosper for it. And we want to lash out against them.

We must be very careful in our responses to the wicked things going on. We need to focus on the unjust and sinful actions and not vent our anger on individuals. It's often said we should hate the sin but love the sinner. That may sound simple, but it's incredibly difficult. Only God can love perfectly and hate perfectly without contradiction. We cannot hate people when we disagree, even when they behave in sinful ways. We should hate the injustice and sinfulness of the acts they are perpetuating. But we cannot respond with violence.

Someone right now is reading this and asking, "But what about Jesus? Didn't He overturn the money changers' tables and drive them out of the temple with a whip? Why can't we do what Jesus did?!" First, we need to consider what Jesus did in the temple. The money changers in the temple were cheating people and keeping people from worshiping God.

Jesus was driven by righteous anger and appropriate zeal for God's holiness. He put a stop to the wicked actions of the people profaning the temple. But He was not violent with the people in the temple. Jesus consistently showed mercy and forgiveness toward individuals. He treated them with respect and compassion, even when He knew their hearts were set against Him.

Jesus knew Judas was going to betray Him, and He still washed his feet. He asked the Father to forgive the people crucifying Him. Jesus knew people's hearts and had both the ability and the authority to judge them. And this is the biggest difference between Jesus and us. He's God, and we're not.

The Apostle Paul was stoned, persecuted, chased out of town, imprisoned, and eventually killed for his faith. But he never retaliated, and he encouraged believers to live peacefully and not seek revenge. The bottom line is that from the Old Testament to the New Testament, God is explicitly consistent saying that vengeance is for the Lord. Christians cannot engage in worldly retaliation.

There is a growing movement on the Right, mostly in the post-Christian Right, viewing grace as a sign of weakness. Its adherents want to grab power back by behaving like the Left. Some want a national-populist movement of one-size-fits-all morality and a government-imposed determination of what is in people's best interests and morals.

None seems to have a real path forward other than puffery— casting blame, decrying the conservatism they think has failed them, and demanding a rejection of everything that actually got them to where they are. They have internalized the American decline in the same way as so many of the establishment politicians of both parties have. Their ideas amount to dividing the spoils of what was and stockpiling to prepare for dystopia.

In November 2020, the American public rejected President Trump's puffed-up rage machine and also rejected the Democrats' puffed-up rage machine. The American public embraced *stability*. Faced with a reckless president, Americans embraced a boring old man who promised normalcy. Faced with defunding the police and with socialists, the American people almost gave Republicans back the House of Representatives while adding more GOP power at the state level. It was Republicans filled with despair and a loss of hope who gave up and handed the United States Senate to the Democrats.

A Rightwing message of "own the Left through any means" and "the Constitution is broken" belongs to keyboard warriors and political losers. Dabbling in authoritarian rhetoric and despair is not the winning path. Trusting in the profound wisdom of the American citizen to want another sunrise wins every time.

Good Things, Bad People?

Psalm 73 is my favorite psalm. Asaph wrote it. He was one of the three singers charged by King David with overseeing music in the House of the Lord. Asaph wrote Psalm 73 after becoming envious of the success of the people who were dismissive of God:

> For I was envious of the arrogant when I saw the prosperity of the wicked. For they have no pangs until death; their bodies are fat and sleek. They are not in trouble as others are; they are not stricken like the rest of mankind. Therefore pride is their necklace; violence covers them as a garment. Their eyes swell out through fatness; their hearts overflow with follies. They scoff and speak with malice; loftily they threaten oppression. They set their mouths against the heavens, and their tongue struts through the earth. (Psalm 73:3–9, ESV)

Asaph saw how sinful and unjust the wicked were, and yet, they didn't suffer for it. They prospered. They were strong and well-fed. They had every outward appearance of success. Did they credit God for their success? Did they praise and thank Him? No! They were filled with pride in themselves and scorn for God. Were they kind and generous toward others? No! They were filled with violence, malice, and oppression. These were horrible people doing terrible deeds.

Can you see the similarities between those arrogant and wicked people and the godless pagans who mock God and His people today? I don't know about you, but I find great comfort reading Asaph's words. The wicked have always seemed successful and popular. There is nothing new under heaven.

Like many of us, Asaph was jealous of the wicked and their success. He couldn't figure out how to reconcile their success with God's holiness and justice. But look at what he says next:

> But when I thought how to understand this, it
> seemed to me a wearisome task, until I went into
> the sanctuary of God; then I discerned their end.
> Truly you set them in slippery places; you make
> them fall to ruin. How they are destroyed in a
> moment, swept away utterly by terrors! (Psalm
> 73:16–19, ESV)

Asaph realized the wicked won't always prosper. Ultimately, they will be destroyed and ruined. God sees, and He is not mocked. But He is God, and we are not. Vengeance is His, not ours. Asaph ends Psalm 73 with these words of encouragement: "For behold, those who are far from you shall perish; you put an end to everyone who is unfaithful to you. But for me it is good to be near God; I have made the Lord God my refuge, that I may tell of all your works." (Psalm 73:27–28, ESV) When God is your refuge, you can trust that He will continue to hold all things together. For those of us who have put our trust in Him, we can trust that His justice will prevail and that our ultimate success is assured in Christ. Knowing that the future is secure, we can let go of retaliation and vengeance and focus on positive steps to be salt and light in our communities.

Be the Light

Think about how David treated Saul. David had been anointed as God's choice as the next king. But Saul was still king over Israel. Saul hated David and tried to kill him several times. Hurled a spear at him. Insulted him and mistreated him. Schemed to get rid of him.

David's best friend was Jonathan, Saul's son and likely heir. By all accounts they should have hated each other. But they didn't. Scripture says that Jonathan intervened to save David's life. David ended up hiding in the wilderness with his loyal men, and Saul went after him with his army.

David wrote several psalms during his time in the wilderness. Psalms 57 and 142 were both written in a cave. David's life was at stake, and he turned to God to rescue him. Twice, David had the opportunity to kill Saul. Both times he refused to take advantage of the circumstances. David showed Saul the mercy and forgiveness that Saul never showed or deserved. He never retaliated against Saul.

In Psalm 18, written after God rescued David from Saul, David praises God:

> The Lord is my rock and my fortress and my
> deliverer, my God, my rock, in whom I take

refuge, my shield, and the horn of my salvation,
my stronghold. I call upon the Lord, who is worthy to be praised, and I am saved from my enemies. (Psalm 18:2–3, ESV)

God is our rock, fortress, deliverer, refuge, shield, and salvation, just like He was for David. When we are attacked by our
enemies, we can respond with grace.

At the beginning of the COVID-19 pandemic, two boys in
middle Georgia were selling crosses as part of a "faith over fear"
campaign. The proceeds went to buy snacks for hospital break
rooms. Since people couldn't go to church on Easter, they put up
crosses in their yards to celebrate and encourage others. Many
people decorated the crosses with lights or shone spotlights on
them. Getting into the spirit of things, I pulled out the Christmas
lights, wrapped the cross up like several of my neighbors had
done, and put a picture on Instagram.

And then all hell broke loose.

Trolls on the internet accused me of burning a cross in my
own yard. *Newsweek* sprang into action claiming, "Conservative
Radio Host Erick Erickson Criticized for Placing 'Burning Cross'
in Front Yard."[131]

While Christians were focused on the Resurrection of Christ
that year, I was reminded: The world still hates us. Pagans were
mad because someone wrapped Christmas lights around an Easter
cross to remind people of the light shining in the darkness. They

---

[131] Benjamin Fearnow, "Conservative Radio Host Erick Erickson Accused of
Racial Insensitivity for Putting Lights on Cross in His Yard," *Newsweek*,
April 5, 2020, https://www.newsweek.com/conservative-radio-host-er-
ick-erickson-criticized-placing-burning-cross-front-yard-1496196

wanted to shame me and silence others. How did I respond? I bought extra lights to make the cross shine brighter.

The world continues to turn and nothing has changed. The world has never liked or understood Christians. It is far easier to impute bad motives to someone than show him grace, because grace is a particular trait of Christianity not shared by other religions.

What is true right now is that Christians need to be the light. We should be far more focused on the Resurrection, and not just on Sundays and Easter. And we should be willing to extend grace even when it isn't returned to us.

Jesus entered Jerusalem as the crowds shouted, "Hosanna!" He finished the week spit upon, beaten, tortured, nailed to a cross, and killed. Throughout it all, He blessed people, even on the way to Golgotha. Christian, how can you be a blessing? God has given you gifts. Ignore the angry world. Show grace. Be the light.

Diversify Your Media Diet

One of the practical steps you can take to protect yourself from the outrage machine is to widen your sources. All media outlets are biased, some more than others. The bias is not so much in what the media cover, but what they *don't* cover. It can be hard to see the bias because you simply don't see the stories or the relevant angle they choose not to report.

When Donald Rumsfeld was secretary of defense, he talked about the known knowns, the known unknowns, the unknown knowns, and the things you don't know you know. Most dangerous of all were the unknown unknowns, the things you don't know you don't know. That is the key to understanding the bias across the entirety of news media. By avoiding stories or details or angles, they leave you thinking that you're well-informed and that you've been given the full picture. But you don't know what you're missing.

News is like any other entertainment business. The news outlets need subscriptions, ratings, and ad revenue. In order to keep you coming back, they leave out key information or don't cover certain stories to present you with information that affirms what you already believe.

You can't rely on one source of news. Don't just watch Fox News, don't just watch MSNBC, don't just watch CNN. Flip between them, for example, CNN and Fox. Read *National Review*, but also read *The New York Times*. Listen to multiple voices on a subject, especially those with different points of view. So, listen to Fox News, but also try to find CNN's coverage of the same thing. It's not going to convert you into a liberal by listening to CNN, but you may hear additional details that Fox News didn't cover. Sometimes, as stories develop, information isn't intentionally left out, but more details become available over time.

For my show prep, I read everything. I read Left, I read Right, I read Center. I try to contact first-hand sources, if possible, to get their take. That's not something everyone can do, I realize. But anyone can diversify his media diet. And it's important that we all do.

Which brings me to the next point about news media. Too much news isn't healthy for anyone. You've got to unplug. Never react abruptly to breaking news. Wait a few days and see how the story develops. Be mindful when you hear a news story to go back later and see how it unfolded. Very often the news story is different from the day it first broke. It takes discipline to be well-informed. You can't depend on a particular source to tell you all you need to know. You have to research and continue to follow up with the stories.

I used to do what much of the media does, and in response to so much of the media doing what it does now, I've changed. My approach now is to inform people, especially the silent majority caught in the middle. The who, what, where, and how. I don't tell you what to believe; my goal is to give you all the information you need to think for yourself.

As the media play to increasingly extreme sides, I don't want to play to any side, even though I'm conservative. I want liberals to be able to listen to me and come away with a better understanding of what's going on. While I have strongly held beliefs in many areas, I want to be as approachable as possible to everybody. I just want to tell people, "Here's what's happening in the world. I'll tell you what I think about it as a Christian conservative," but I don't want to leave out key facts to shape the story.

The news media need an audience, and it serves their interests to keep you engaged and enraged so you keep coming back for your next rage fix. The Left and the Right craft a narrative so you will be provoked. They want you anxious and fearful, because the anxiety and fear drive you back to them for a solution to the anxiety they've created. Take a step back from the outrage machine and slow down. Don't give in to the tyranny of the urgent. Things aren't sunshine and roses, but they aren't as bad as the news would have you think.

Change Takes Time

Did you think that *Roe v. Wade* would ever be overturned? When Justice Samuel Alito's draft opinion in *Dobbs v. Jackson Women's Health* was leaked, pro-life conservatives celebrated the end of *Roe v. Wade*. In a five-to-four majority, the U.S. Supreme Court struck down *Roe* and returned the matter to the democratic processes of state legislatures. The decision made clear that abortion is not, and has never been, a constitutional right.

Even Justice Ruth Bader-Ginsburg argued that *Roe* had been terribly decided, though she supported it. *Roe* was always a terrible decision for many reasons. Constitutionally, not morally, the most egregious issue was the Court seeking to cut off debate on an issue about which there were vehement objections and no clear constitutional issue. No person can read the Constitution and find a right to abortion. Worse, abortion was premised on a right to privacy that is itself not in the Constitution, but derived from the Fourth Amendment. Abortion, as a right, is several degrees removed from the Constitution, which meant it should have stayed with the state legislatures, allowing the people to decide state by state.

Abortion in the United States has not been banned. It will go back to the states and state legislatures, a number of which have passed laws to ratify abortion on demand and a number of which have passed laws to ban it. Federalism was always the solution.

It wasn't a quick process, though. It took fifty years to reverse *Roe v. Wade*. The pro-life movement followed the rule of law to accomplish this goal. Its members elected Republican presidents and pushed for pro-life judges. They elected Republican senators who approved those judges and justices. Ironically, it was the Democrats' own rule-breaking that got the *Dobbs* case across the finish line. Had Harry Reid and the Democrats not ended the filibuster for nominations, this moment would not have come. Their rule-breaking ended *Roe*. Pro-lifers followed the rules and were able to capitalize on the Democrats rewriting the rules. Ironic, isn't it?

Most people outside of hardcore partisans and press corps members are not pro-abortion voters, and the end of *Roe* will not make them pro-abortion voters. Already, in many pro-life states, abortion clinics are rare or nonexistent. In progressive states, things will continue as if the decision never happened.

We have won a significant victory, but the battle goes on. The challenge for pro-lifers will continue to be changing people's pro-abortion mindset and helping mothers and their babies. The effort to turn our culture away from the new Gnosticism of the quasi-religious Left will take time. We can't grow discouraged and either give up or give in to violence and revenge. It's like planting trees. If you plant a tree today, water it and care for it over time; it'll be your grandchildren and great-grandchildren who benefit from the shade. As you work diligently for a better future, do it for them.

There are encouraging signs that the tide may be turning. Take, for example, Basecamp, a company in Silicon Valley, which has never really embraced Silicon Valley culture. Google set the standard for Silicon Valley companies by not paying as much as other companies but offering impressive stock options, making it possible to become a millionaire through stock growth. Google also provided extraordinary benefits including gym access, gourmet food, car service, and housing.

Google was essentially saying that if you work at Google, the company will provide for your every need. It only asks that you pour your whole self into the company. If you're giving your all to Google, you want Google to look like you. This is human nature.

The result is that Google hired a bunch of progressive, secular, hyper-liberals who continued to turn the company to the Left. Over time, the company became extremely unwelcoming to people who disagreed. Today Google is a hyper-woke company that is simply not receptive to conservatives. Google employees confirm that they can shape the algorithm—and have—to provide information reflecting their views and not conservative views.

Basecamp, however, has had enough. Basecamp has essentially said that while work is an important part of your life, the company doesn't want to be *all* of your life. Basecamp has pushed its team members to leave their political views at the door and simply focus on the product without leaving "their" mark on it. One of the owners of the company tweeted, "Stop looking to work to fulfill every human emotional need. The reason you're so desperate to cast the company as a family is probably because you've been spending far too much time there. Get away from the office, diversify your life, let work just be one part of it."[132]

Of course, Basecamp is getting excoriated. Even some of its employees have announced they're leaving. If these employees are not allowed to air their political views at the office, they don't want to be in the office. They don't feel it's a family anymore.

Here's the thing, it was never supposed to be a family. Google and other major Silicon Valley companies essentially moved people

---

[132] David Heinemeier Hansson, Twitter post, July 22, 2020, 11:33 a.m., https://twitter.com/dhh/status/1285961254918483973.

from their college campus to their corporate campus and kept many of the college amenities. Instead of going to class, they were going to work.

Basecamp is refusing to treat its employees like college students, and, more important, it is refusing to let its employees' political preferences dictate who can use its products. More of this, please.

Business analyst Ben Thompson wrote:

> Basecamp has defined itself in opposition to the Silicon Valley mindset, and one of its missions is to make it clear that startup culture becomes all-encompassing and people pour themselves into the business, including their political views, and it disrupts their work-life balance and their work becomes their life, and therefore it must reflect their political views and everything else. And it is alienating and marginalizing to people.[133]

He's right. I wonder if we are seeing the beginning of a trend. Basecamp is a relatively small company that's quite influential in the tech community. By saying that it is done with wokeness and wanting employees to act like grownups, will other companies follow? This could be a trend, and it would be a really good trend.

---

[133] Ben Thompson, "Basecamp's New Policy, Basecamp Versus Silicon Valley, Stripe Changes Vesting Schedule," Stratechery, April 27, 2021, https://stratechery.com/2021/basecamps-new-policy-basecamp-versus-silicon-valley-stripe-changes-vesting-schedule/.

Do Not Put Your Trust in Politics

For what does it profit a man to gain the
whole world and forfeit his soul? For what
can a man give in return for his soul?
—Mark 8:36-37 (ESV)

As political parties sort themselves out, we tend to pick sides. Those of us of faith need to remember that our *side* is with Jesus, not Republicans or Democrats. A lot of people on the Right are going to advocate methods, tactics, and positions that may gain you an America you love while costing you eternity. You'll be bullied and harassed for rejecting those methods, tactics, and positions, but you must resist.

Don't put your trust in people, particularly the proud and puffed up. We live in a postmodern world, and there will be those who act like jackasses, and expect jackassery from you toward those on the "other side." You must first love your neighbor. You must show grace.

Frankly and truthfully, we are reaching a time when Christians may have to step out of party politics and maybe out of a party altogether. One of the great dangers of a Republican Party that increasingly covets centralized power is this: Christians know how this story ends. Things are going to get far worse before they get better. Be wary of giving power to any person or tribe which can then be used against you.

A great many people are going to fall away from the church before the final day. It won't just be atheist progressives, but a lot of people in church pews today. Christianity is not compatible with our postmodern age because Christianity is a religion of objective truth. It will survive the age because it is true. But we must continue to make our "yes" a "yes" without giving into peer pressure to go along with the political flow.

Many faithful people will get distracted from eternity in the coming years fighting short-term battles that they will ultimately lose against a godless world. Show them and everyone else a lot of grace. Don't make your friendships dependent on a political tribe. If your friendship is grounded in a shared political community, it's going to be hard to remain friends when you inevitably realize you no longer see eye to eye, even with long-time friends.

Lastly, get offline. The echo chamber and confirmation bias online make us more likely to connect with those who look and think just like us. It isolates us. It hurts our witness, builds our anxieties, and makes us wallow in worry.

Let not your heart be troubled. The God of all creation is on your side. You depend on no party or politician when the King of Glory Himself is leading you. In the next few chapters, we will look at practical ways we can love our neighbors and seek the welfare of our communities.

CHAPTER 8

LOVE YOUR NEIGHBOR

The efforts spent on defending our turf
in the culture wars could be better served
on loving our neighbor as ourselves.
—Allen Yeh

Between the 2020 presidential election and the COVID-19 pandemic, the political and cultural divide in our country has become a chasm dwarfing the Grand Canyon. There often seems to be no way to bridge the gap between the sides. We've grown so used to the rancor and fighting it makes any random act of kindness surprising, if not jarring.

Virginia Heffernan, a columnist for the *Los Angeles Times*, wrote about her dilemma after her MAGA neighbor plowed the snow from her driveway.[134] Heffernan didn't know how to respond

---

[134] Virginia Heffernan, "What Can You Do About the Trumpites Next Door?" *Los Angeles Times*, February 5, 2021, https://www.latimes.com/opinion/story/2021-02-05/trumpite-neighbor-unity-capitol-attack.

to what she called "this act of aggressive niceness." Politically, culturally, socially, she had nothing in common with her neighbor. She realized she should thank him for his kindness and generosity, but she worried how her thanks would be perceived and how it would change their relationship: "When someone helps you when you're down, or snowed in, it's almost impossible to regard them as a blight on the world. In fact, you're more likely to be overwhelmed with gratitude and convinced of the person's inherent goodness."[135]

Would acknowledging her neighbor's kindness make her willing to excuse or forget his connection to Trump and the politics she abhors? Would it make her an ally for his cause? She summarized her internal conflict profoundly, "Loving your neighbor is evidently much easier when your neighborhood is full of people just like you." And all God's people said, "Amen."

It's easier to hate others when you see them as one-dimensional caricatures. Instead of actual human beings, they serve as living embodiments of everything you despise about the other side. When you get to know people as your neighbors, you see them as complex and contradictory. We are all a mixture of good and evil. No one has completely pure motivations. And no one is entirely evil. After all, presidents from both parties love their dogs.

Heffernan ended her article willing to make amends with the other side *if* they work with her side to do what *she* believes is right. In her mindset, there are only two categories of people: allies and enemies.

---

[135] Ibid.

Who Is My Neighbor?

When Jesus was teaching, a lawyer stood up and questioned Him. The lawyer wanted to test Jesus and see if His answers would agree with Scripture. So he asked Jesus what he had to do to inherit eternal life. Jesus responded with a question of His own: "What does the law say?" The lawyer answered by summarizing the Old Testament commands: "You shall love the Lord your God with all your heart and with all your soul and with all your strength and with all your mind, and your neighbor as yourself." When Jesus commended him for his answer, the lawyer asked his next question: "Who is my neighbor?"

The lawyer wanted to prove his own righteousness, but to do so, the meaning of neighbor had to be limited. Jesus answered with the parable of the Good Samaritan:

> A man was going down from Jerusalem to Jericho, and he fell among robbers, who stripped him and beat him and departed, leaving him half dead. Now by chance a priest was going down that road, and when he saw him he passed by on the other side. So likewise a Levite, when he came to the place and saw him, passed by on the other side. But a Samaritan, as he journeyed, came to where he was, and when he saw him, he had compassion. He went to him and bound up his wounds, pouring on oil and wine. Then he set him on his own animal and brought him to an inn and took care of him. And the next day he took out two denarii and gave them to the

> innkeeper, saying, "Take care of him, and what-
> ever more you spend, I will repay you when I
> come back." (Luke 10:30–35, ESV)

Jesus finished the parable by asking which of the three people was a neighbor to the injured man. The lawyer replied that the neighbor was the one who showed the man mercy. Jesus told the lawyer to go and do as the Samaritan had done.

The Good Samaritan is one of the most famous parables. In it, the religious people avoid a man in a ditch who had been set upon by robbers. But the Samaritan, from a group of people hated and despised by Jewish society, showed love and mercy to the man in the ditch and took care of him.

For today's audience, Jesus might have made the characters an evangelical preacher and a GOP politician who passed by the injured man. The hero of the story might have been a Democrat with a "Coexist" sticker on her car. The point of the parable is not which group each person belongs to, but how they treat each other. The Samaritan did not ask if the person was from his town or shared his faith, or if he was straight, gay, transgender, or anything else. He just showed brotherly love.

Two thousand years later, we are still arguing over who our neighbors are and what we owe them. We divide ourselves by politics, culture, and religion. If my neighbors don't agree with me, well, I don't want to know them. I certainly don't want to have to show them love and mercy as my neighbors or brothers.

In our isolated and segmented culture, we rarely even know the people who live near us. Some of you live in an apartment complex or in town homes. You likely don't even know the person on the other side of the wall from you. Or maybe you're in a neigh-borhood like me where I can see out my window to the houses across the street, but you don't know the people who live there. What about the gay guy across the street with the Hillary Clinton sign still in his yard, or the Joe Biden sign—is he my neighbor?

The people living near you are your immediate neighbors, whatever their politics. And the poor families who live in the next town are your neighbors as well. So is the homeless guy on the street.

When I see a homeless guy on the street, I'm not the per-son who wants to roll down my window and give him money. I'm really not. I don't like to do it. It's awkward, and I wonder if the money will be used to buy drugs and alcohol.

I was convinced recently by a lady to think about it differently. She said to roll my window down and give the guy standing there five bucks. Yeah, you might just be giving someone money so he can buy drugs, but how can you be sure? Isn't it better to err on the side of helping someone who might really be in need? If I'm taken advantage of when I can afford to be, isn't that better than denying someone a meal when his family is starving?

I had never thought about it that way. I'm not saying you have to give money to every person you see on the side of the road. It's a matter for you to decide. I admit I still sometimes hesitate and, in any event, rarely have cash on me. What I am saying is, like the Good Samaritan, we should be willing to be inconvenienced if it means helping others. People all around you are struggling in dif-ferent ways. Show them mercy. Be a good neighbor. Even if they don't deserve it.

Why Should We Love Our Neighbor?

As we've been discussing, the secular religion of the Left has no concept of grace. If mercy is sparing others from something they deserve, grace is giving others something they do not deserve. Grace is a uniquely Christian concept.

In the Christian doctrine of Salvation, if you repent and trust in Christ, you are saved whether or not anyone else repents. Everyone else around you may go to hell, but you will spend eternity with Christ. In the new Gnosticism where the mob is god, though you yourself may repent, you are still damned as long as there are unrepentant sinners out there.

Let's say, for example, you repent of your belief that climate change is nonsense, and accept that mankind is to blame. You trade in your car for a bike. You unplug your home from the power grid and install solar panels and a windmill. You invest in unicorn farts for extra power. You also take up composting and a religious devotion to recycling.

You are still damned to a hell on Earth as long as your neighbor continues driving his SUV, having more than 2.25 kids, and burning incandescent light bulbs. He must be punished, re-educated, silenced, or driven from society in order for you to be saved.

The same holds true with transgenderism. Let's say you finally give up the quaint scientific theory stating that boys cannot become girls and instead embrace the Leftist dogma that we are born gay or straight and get to choose our own gender. If even one Christian bigot is out there saying otherwise, you cannot have heaven on Earth. The bigots must be censored, silenced, driven from society, or worse.

But we know better. We have received mercy, grace, forgiveness, and love. And we didn't deserve it. The Scriptures teach us Christ died for us even though we were sinners and enemies of God. And because we have been shown grace and love, we are called to love others, even our enemies:

> Love your enemies, do good to those who hate you, bless those who curse you, pray for those who abuse you. To one who strikes you on the cheek, offer the other also, and from one who takes away your cloak do not withhold your tunic either. Give to everyone who begs from you, and from one who takes away your goods do not demand them back. And as you wish that others would do to you, do so to them. If you love those who love you, what benefit is that to you? For even sinners do the same... But love your enemies, and do good, and lend, expecting nothing in return... Be merciful, even as your Father is merciful. (Luke 6:27–32, 35–36, ESV)

We don't live like other people do. We have a higher standard to uphold. We are loved by God, and so we love others. We even do good to those who persecute us:

> Bless those who persecute you; bless and do not curse them... Repay no one evil for evil... If possible, so far as it depends on you, live peaceably with all. Beloved, never avenge yourselves, but leave it to the wrath of God, for it is

written, "Vengeance is mine, I will repay, says the Lord." To the contrary, "if your enemy is hungry, feed him; if he is thirsty, give him something to drink; for by so doing you will heap burning coals on his head." Do not be overcome by evil, but overcome evil with good. (Romans 12:14, 17–21, ESV)

I'm not saying it's easy. It's very hard to love people who hate you. But loving others is the way to overcome evil.

What Does it Mean to Love Others?

How awesome would it be if, in a time
of need, the first thing people would
say is, "I need a Christian!"
—Thom Schultz

Republican Sharon Cooper is a representative in the Georgia legislature. She chairs the Public Health Committee which recently considered a bill to ban hormone therapy and gender transition surgeries for minors. Before the committee voted, Cooper expressed her wish of having another bill to protect transgender people, including children, from discrimination. After the vote advancing the bill, Cooper was seen hugging a mother of a transgender child.[136]

---

[136] Wendy Parker, "East Cobb Legislator Excused from Voting on Transgender Bill," *East Cobb News*, March 16, 2023, https://eastcobbnews.com/east-cobb-legislator-excused-from-voting-on-transgender-bill/.

Was her comforting a hurting mother an example of loving others? Not according to many critics online. From some of the Twitter responses:

> "SHAME on @RepSharonCooper for creating this situation!"[137]

> "If you vote for a bill that hurts trans kids, you don't get to try and comfort the mothers of trans kids."[138]

Many even questioned why the mother would be willing to hug the person they view as responsible for the bill advancing. In our culture, the prevailing belief is that love means giving people what they want. Loving your neighbor is a deeply confused concept for people on both sides of the political divide.

When it comes to loving your neighbor, we tend to misunderstand the lessons of Genesis. The Left gets Genesis 1 and 2 wrong, and the Right gets Genesis 3 and 4 wrong. In Genesis 1 and 2, we find the confirmation of biblical sexuality right there in the creation story. It's funny to read Christians on the Left arguing over what God's pronouns should be. The Left claims everyone should get to pick their gender. Well, God already picked, why can't we recognize the Creator's pronouns? He created gender, for Pete's sake.

There's also a lack of understanding by the Right. In Genesis 4, Cain asks, "Am I my brother's keeper?" There are a number

---

[137] Drewbob404, Twitter post, March 15, 2023, 12:54 p.m., https://twitter.com/BAndrewPlant/status/1636063345575964681.

[138] Nevermet, Twitter post, March 17, 2023, 5:04 p.m., https://twitter.com/NicktheNevermet/status/1636851051499343876.

of Christians who think the answer is, "No, I'm not my brother's keeper." But that's not right. Yes, you are your brother's keeper. And like the meaning of "neighbor," it doesn't just mean your biological brother or family, it means the people around you, in your community and around the world. You're supposed to take care of other people.

Pastor and author Timothy Keller defines love as being willing to take care of someone in a sacrificial way. Just as Jesus was willing to die for us, we need to be willing to be inconvenienced for the sake of others, even those who disagree with us.[139] And it can be something so minor as having to go across the street to make sure the neighbor's cat has food when he is out of town.

Part of loving your neighbor is simply helping out. It can also be helping someone you don't know who is suffering in some way. I had a similar situation when I was on the city council. A member of council, who was adamantly opposed to me on all things, had her home burned down. My wife and I cooked the family a meal and took it to their hotel so they wouldn't have to eat out. Just one week later, the council member was in the newspaper referring to my family in unkind ways. Would I have changed what we did, knowing she would continue to treat me as an enemy? No. Regardless of her reciprocal nature or not, we wanted to show her and her family love as our neighbors.

Some on the Right equate loving their neighbor with confronting people with their sins and demanding they repent. After all, it's loving to want them not to go to hell, right? But that attitude

---

[139] Timothy Keller, "Hope in Times of Fear," interview with Erick Erickson, Erick Erickson Show, podcast audio, April 2, 2021, https://ewerickson.substack.com/p/hope-in-times-of-fear.

misses the point. If you don't have a relationship with someone, he will never change his mind just because you yell at him to repent.

You aren't the Holy Spirit. You can't make someone repent. But if you develop a relationship with someone, become a good neighbor to that person, God may use you and your relationship to work in that person's life. And remember, in Genesis 3, we see Jesus is going to crush the head of the serpent. We don't have to worry about how this is all going to end. He's got this covered.

On the Left, people think that loving your neighbor means you have to embrace the totality of a person and all his sins, particularly sexual sins. On the Right, people think that loving your neighbors means yelling at them to repent on a daily basis and exposing all of their sins. Both sides need to recognize that loving your neighbor means following the Golden Rule: Do unto others as you would have them do unto you. You want to be someone your neighbor can rely on.

Being Nice Is for Sissies!

> Love the Lord your God with all your heart
> and with all your soul and with all your
> mind and with all your strength... Love
> your neighbor as yourself. There is no other
> commandment greater than these.
> —Mark 12:30, 31, ESV

I have studied this passage in multiple English translations. I've read it in the original Greek from the Alexandrian-type codex, the Byzantine Textus Receptus, and other versions. I cannot find footnotes, caveats, provisos, or exceptions. We are supposed to love our neighbors whether they are black, white, gay, straight, transgender, conservative, or progressive.

We have reached an unfortunate point where people who are nice are mocked as losers. Being nice or civil is now a sign of weakness. Having friends across the aisle is, too. We can't turn the other cheek or love our neighbors if they disagree with us. Loving our gay neighbors now means we have to stand in the yard and tell them they're going to burn in hell.

We're not relational people anymore. We're too "online" for such things. Relationships are weaknesses. Loving your neighbor might mean you have to actually get to know someone in the real world and find out you disagree on something. It's all mean tweets all the time instead. "It's war!" people tweet from the comfort of their couches or offices or cars without ever, in real life, acting like it.

We've all seemingly lost the plot of the only narrative that matters. Society itself reflects this. The most popular shows reflect the nihilism of the age. *Game of Thrones* famously killed off anyone you cared about before killing off how much you care about the show with a ridiculous finale. *Succession* highlights the foibles of a billionaire family of terrible people. The secret to understanding the show, a media critic pointed out, was to understand that in *Succession* each person gets what he wants and is more miserable because of it. Other networks have followed with many new shows designed to make you hate everyone in the show.

As real religion has given way to politics, religious orthodoxy now is wrapped around political beliefs and partisan interpretations of events. With no grace in the political religion, there's just rage, jackassery, and bullying anyone who dissents into silence.

Cancel culture thrives on all sides. Anyone and anything sincere, good, and true is laughed at and mocked by all sides as weak.

The Left has no mercy for anyone who points out that maybe dissenters have a point. Leftists bullied Patton Oswald, the comedian, into apologizing for being friends with Dave Chappelle. Gen Z and younger millennial progressives may idolize Harry Potter, but they were quick to cancel its creator because she dared to truthfully say that men cannot become women. Having canceled the actual Creator, they'll cancel anyone who affirms His creation design.

Anyone who says anything you disagree with must have his motives questioned. We don't treat anyone charitably. We assume everyone has an angle or an agenda. We impute bad motives instead of just disagreeing. Postmodernism has us all in its clutches.

Kindness and gentleness aren't weaknesses. They're the fruit of the Spirit: "The fruit of the Spirit is love, joy, peace, patience, kindness, goodness, faithfulness, gentleness, self-control." (Galatians 5:22–23, ESV)

Christian, we can't be like the world, or we won't reflect Christ. It is hard. The temptation to tribalism pulls at all of us. But we are not a tribe. We are the church, and we must put our trust in Him, not our own efforts.

Above all else, we must show each other grace. We must allow each other to speak into the world and culture in Spirit and truth without condemnation for others doing gospel-centered tasks in a way we might not.

Christianity requires us to not ridicule others in the church and resist sending the tribal mob off to enforce matters where Christians may disagree. Not everything you dislike is disliked by God, and God will not find fault in everything you do.

Our ways are not the world's ways. I am convinced social media (specifically Twitter) is harming our ability to show each other grace. In matters of conscience, Christians have liberty, as long as it doesn't undermine the orthodoxy of the church.

As I said earlier, we need the ways of Mary and of Martha and the differing views and passions of the various Apostles. We need Jesus above all else. "Now the Lord is the Spirit, and where the Spirit of the Lord is, there is freedom." (2 Corinthians 3:17, ESV)

Everyone has forgotten how this story ends, and we're miserable and unkind because of it. It has a happy ending, and it all ends with the king returning. Y'all, if you're on the winning team, maybe start acting like it. The story has a happy ending, so you can be happy, too.

Being mean because you might lose some tribal power is wasted energy. When Jesus returns, He will clean it all up and make all things new and perfect and good. Society may have lost the plot, but we shouldn't.

Friends with Sinners

A recent study showed that conservatives tend to have more friends who are liberal than liberals have conservative friends. *The Washington Post* ran a story about the study that opened with an anecdote about a liberal who had to abandon his friendship with a conservative who went down the QAnon rabbit hole. The story failed to grasp the real reasons behind the study's results.[140]

---

[140] Lisa Bonos, "Republicans Have More Friends Across the Political Divide than Democrats, Study Finds," *The Washington Post*, July 3, 2021, https://www.washingtonpost.com/lifestyle/2021/07/03/how-politics-divides-friends/.

First, liberals in America today tend to live in enclaves with other liberals. Conservatives tend to commute to more liberal areas for work. A liberal in San Francisco might go a full day without encountering a conservative, but a conservative in Atlanta would have a hard time not encountering a liberal.

Second, a growing number of liberals have substituted faith for politics to fulfill their souls. Substituting politics for religion pollutes the soul. The Left's retreat from Christianity into the new Gnosticism ends badly for a lot of people. Protests will never fill the soul like the Holy Spirit can. Casting out those who refuse to embrace the idol of the day leaves no room for grace and forgiveness. Eventually, there's a new idol of the day, and the liberal is either forced to keep up or realize that now he, too, is a heretic in an environment where grace has no home.

It's true that God hates sin. But the very same God not only hung out with sinners and befriended them, He also died on a cross for their sins. The very sins of the people He befriended caused Him to be tortured, beaten to within an inch of His life, and nailed to a cross.

Jesus built real friendships with sinners and through those relationships, His friends repented and accepted Him. He meaningfully loved His neighbors so He could share His good news. Do you hate sin so much more than God that you can't be friends with the person whose views you think will destroy your country—not your eternal home?

If so, your sin of pride adds to your pile while you disdain a helping hand to the sinner across the street because they sin differently from you, and you hate their sin more than your own sins. Jesus, on the cross, wishes He could have had your self-righteousness.

Liberals have traditionally had this problem way more than conservatives. They truly cannot love their neighbor if their neighbor holds views that they despise. The data has shown this for years, and it has gotten more pronounced in the past decade as the new Gnosticism replaces Christianity.

But as politics gets more visceral and more all-encompassing, increasingly many churchgoing, Bible-believing conservatives are behaving more and more like the Left. They don't want to have friendships with those with whom they have political disagreements. They don't trust others who are willing to have those friendships. And they make copious excuses for why and how they don't have to love certain neighbors. Or they twist loving their neighbor into jackassery so they can get out of God's commandment.

"Love your neighbor" gives you no loophole for jackassery. It gives no permission to avoid your fellow sinners because you disdain their sins. Jesus was friends with those whose sins sent Him to the grave. If you can't be friends with people because you think their political views are destroying your country, you're not only behaving exactly like the Left, but you're also making an idol of a temporary place and putting it ahead of God's direct command to love your neighbor.

Romans 12:2 says, "Do not be conformed to this world, but be transformed by the renewal of your mind." What it's really saying is, be careful not to let the thought categories of this world control your faith.

In Christ, we need to care for others, especially those in need. We can't cede the responsibility to care for others to the Left simply because it claims to care for the poor. As Christians, we have to ask ourselves: Are we letting the Bible dictate our agenda, or are we letting the world's politics dictate it?

When the world says you can't be friends with people who disagree with you, Jesus showed us how to be friends with sinners. Jesus, Paul, and Peter taught the early Christians to be counter-cultural, to go against the cultural trends. So, while the current culture is brash and in your face, you're quiet and modest. As the current culture is sexually licentious, you're not. When the current culture rages about everything, you smile and have inner peace. And as the world shuns those whom they disagree with, you embrace them as friends and love them as neighbors.

Practical Ways to Love Our Neighbors

The story of the Good Samaritan is Jesus's way of telling us to have mercy and compassion for others. Sometimes, we must burden or inconvenience ourselves to protect and take care of others, even strangers among us or those we would not normally get along with. During the COVID-19 pandemic, my wife and I struggled with the decision of sending our children back to school. My wife has lung cancer, which puts her in the category of vulnerable people.

From the beginning of the pandemic, I did five hours of radio a day, got the family fed between shows, and ran the masked gauntlet at grocery stores on the weekend. I did all of it to keep my wife safe. I wore masks when others laughed at me. Friends told me I was overreacting. But even if the pandemic only affected the already medically fragile, my wife *is* medically fragile.

When we could send our kids to school, we knew they would be surrounded by kids whose own parents would not take the same steps to avoid the virus. We wanted our kids to be with their friends and teachers. But that required us to trust each other. Yes, like the good Samaritan, it would require some people to inconvenience themselves, just so others could be safe.

Decisions about how to love our neighbors during the pandemic led to many disagreements and lots of angry words among Americans. Increasingly, Americans hate one another. In the debate over shelter-in-place vs. going back to work, we saw a side of it. We saw two groups concerned about the welfare of Americans and deciding on different approaches and hating those who took the different approach.

The one wanted everyone to stay home to avoid getting sick and overwhelming hospitals. The other wanted everyone who was able and without pre-existing conditions to go back to work lest the mental strain spike suicides and other bad effects. Both came from a position of loving their neighbor.

You can see how religious wars and denominationalism take hold. All sides care about the welfare of others. They all have the same goal. But they split apart and attack the other side's motives. These are not easy issues to navigate. What should be easy, though, are basic understanding, love, and grace.

You can't let anger over disagreements with your neighbors build up over time. You can choose not to be mad at your neighbor. Being mad is increasingly a choice in these sorts of things.

I'm not saying there aren't reasons to be mad. There certainly are. There is a need for righteous indignation as we discussed earlier. But it's your choice to let anger fester or to move on. And just as good fences make good neighbors, so does the willingness not to hold grudges over disagreements. There's room for grace. You have to be willing to agree to disagree.

You live in a society where people don't share your values. When Jesus was telling the disciples to love their neighbors, they lived in a world controlled by a polytheistic Roman Empire. Roman leaders and society approved of awful things. Yet Jesus still told His disciples to love their neighbors, including the neighbor who did not recognize Jesus as Lord. And those who did not share their values and thought these Christians were kind of weird.

Remember, God's in charge. He has a plan and it may not be your plan, but it is the plan. The gates of hell will not prevail. Everything that happens is part of God's plan, and it is bigger than anything we can see or comprehend.

All leaders come to power and leave power as part of God's plan. Through it all, we have an obligation to truth because Jesus is truth and our obligation to Him comes before our obligation to anything else.

He who brought bread from heaven, water from rocks, and raised you from the dust of the Earth and stitched you together in your mother's womb will prepare a table before you in the presence of your enemies. Your cup will overflow. Trust in Him and love your neighbor.

Yeah, even *that* neighbor.

CHAPTER 9

RECONNECT WITH YOUR FAITH

*You can't solve a spiritual problem with
a military or political solution.*
—Jonathan Cahn

In 1815, Johann Maelzel invented the windup metronome. For those not musically inclined: A metronome is a device used to set pacing for music so musicians can keep regular tempo. Metronomes are used to figure out beats per minute. A metronomic life is a life with a tempo—a life with a set pace.

My wife and I live in metronomic regularity with time broken into quarterly visits to a doctor in Atlanta. My wife will get up at sunrise, go to a hospital, offer up several vials of blood, wait patiently for her turn to pass through a CT machine, then wait to meet with her doctor. While waiting, her doctor and a team of oncology professionals will read her lab work and CT scan to determine if her cancer is active.

We do this every three months, a slow-paced tick and tock of a metronomic existence waiting for a shoe to drop—waiting for Damocles' sword to fall.

My wife's lung cancer is genetic. There is no cure. Her lungs are riddled with very small tumors. There are too many to surgically extract, and they are all 5 millimeters or smaller. If she received a lung transplant, the new lungs would eventually develop the tumors.

Her cancer forms due to a protein her body produces. Doctors have invented a pill she takes daily to keep her body from producing the protein. So long as the protein is not produced, the tumors will not grow. One day her body will find a way around the medicine. Each visit we hope the day has not arrived. Thankfully, it has not yet.

In 2006, my wife was given six months to live. She was diagnosed with cancer, and doctors presumed it had spread to her lungs in its final stages. Providentially, they misdiagnosed her. In 2016, as I was being rushed into a cardiac ICU unit trying very hard not to die from blood clots in my lungs, the Mayo Clinic called my wife. Yes, the very same day my body was shutting down because of clots in my lungs, the Mayo Clinic called to tell my wife she had lung cancer.

Had she not been misdiagnosed in 2006, we would have never known about her actual cancer in 2016. Thankfully, they were able to catch it in time and get her into treatment. Again, providentially, one of the world's foremost experts on this type of cancer was just an hour's drive from our home. He is now her doctor.

All of this—my health and my wife's, has changed my perspective on politics. The metronomic regularity of waiting for a shoe to drop has forced me to focus on what really matters. It's also given me a greater awareness of how often my political beliefs have tried to pollute my faith. As I notice others struggling to put their faith into a political box, it strikes me—so much of this is fleeting. People on both sides are trying to build something permanent on shifting, impermanent sand.

The political houses of both parties in this country are built upon the sand. Only people of faith can build their houses on the rock. Sadly, even many of them want to build their houses on the sand, too. They want a heaven on Earth or politicians who can protect us from danger. But nothing in this life is certain except death and taxes, as the saying goes. The other certainty is Jesus's return. When the day comes, it will not matter if you yelled loud enough, passed enough laws, or scored enough points against the other side. What will matter is if you've accepted Jesus as your Lord and Savior.

We Have a Spiritual Problem

Our country doesn't have a partisan problem, a political problem, a social problem, an economic problem, or any other problem as big as the spiritual problem we have. In the absence of God, Americans across partisan lines have turned to government and celebrities. They have gone off to worship idols.

As yet another school shooting dominates the airwaves, news media and politicians on both sides of the aisle are taking turns pointing fingers and blaming others for what happened. Neither side is addressing the spiritual problem at the root.

The president could point people to their churches and communities. The partisans could pause to reflect instead of using a tragedy to advance politics and attack the other side or deflect attacks. They could call on people to denounce evil and look to their communities.

God is not the source of evil. Evil is found in the absence of God. Where God is not, evil is. The American nation, its politicians, and its people have tried to push God out of their lives and evil flourishes in the void they all created.

The Left and Right, even self-described Christians, put party loyalty above loving neighbor and Christ. And evil creeps in. It is destroying families. It is tearing up neighborhoods and communities. It is tearing up the nation.

The school shooter succumbed to the evil of hate—he loved himself more than he loved his neighbor. The partisans will now make it worse and bring more division, more hate, and more strife. Evil will creep further in.

We need Jesus, not partisanship. Our leaders have failed us on all sides. They've led us to idols and performance art on social media, distracting us from our mission: to spread the gospel, love our neighbor, and care for our families.

Many loud voices on the Right seem to think that what we do on Sunday is separate from the other six days of the week. But you can't pray for your enemies on Sunday and decide to punch them on Monday—even if you're sure they're going to punch you otherwise.

Peter, headed toward his execution, told Christians to pray *for* the emperor—not *against* him. Many people today say, "Well, I'm praying for the president to repent and change, or leave me alone, or die." Should we pray for politicians to repent? Of course, but Peter's point was that we should pray that our leaders are authentic instruments of God's will. We should pray for their health and competent leadership. We should *not* be praying for them to get out of our way or die.

Many Christian influencers who are involved in politics are really engaged in performance and platform building. They're trying to build their following by trashing those they disagree with. They can't just disagree—they have to pick a fight and rally a mob. I expect this of the religious Left, but I see it happening among the Right as well.

These influencers are conforming their faith to their politics. When the two diverge, they're slow to speak out about their faith for fear of losing political allies and their platform. Christians in America have had the freedom to practice their religion openly, unlike so many Christians around the world. Because they don't have to be quiet, they've decided to be loud, proud, and belligerent in defense of their faith. Where's the humbleness and the humility?

And where is the grace? The willingness of Christian influencers in politics to ostracize, alienate, shun, and condemn fellow Christians because of political disagreement, not theological disagreement, is growing. These people are not calling others to Christ but to their political tribe. To our shame, we are contributing to our nation's spiritual problem.

The bottom line is this—if you have a platform, and you claim to be a Christian who seeks to be guided by your faith, then you need to remember Christ is more important than a political party. God's kingdom is more important than any nation. Faith and party politics cannot be reconciled. You cannot serve two masters.

If you believe your party and your politics are an accurate reflection of Christ, you've lost sight of what matters most. At some point, you have to recognize that what will matter most is how many people you led to Christ, not to a voting booth.

The constant dragging of authentic, orthodox Christians by evangelicals who disagree with them on political issues is doing nothing but playing into Satan's hands. Politics will never save us and may very well destroy us.

Our Faith Is Not in Politics

> *You sum up the whole of New Testament religion if you describe it as the knowledge of God as one's holy Father. If you want to judge how well a person understands Christianity, find out how much he makes of the thought of being God's child, and having God as his Father. If this is not the thought that prompts and controls his worship and prayers and his whole outlook on life, it means that he does not understand Christianity very well at all... "Father" is the Christian name for God. Our understanding of Christianity cannot be better than our grasp of adoption.*
> —J.I. Packer

Christians in America and, in particular Christians in politics, too often lose sight of our adoption. We want a Daddy Politician to save us. Conservatives who pride themselves on rugged individualism go off and find someone to tell them what to think. Liberals who believe in the collective want the whole world dependent on Uncle Sam.

John Calvin noted, "The human mind is, so to speak, a perpetual forge of idols."[141] What people miss is his further explanation:

> The human mind, stuffed as it is with presumptuous rashness, dares to imagine a god suited to its own capacity… The god whom man has thus conceived inwardly he attempts to embody outwardly. The mind, in this way, conceives the idol, and the hand gives it birth.

The American church and American Christians seem perpetually in pursuit of idol worship.

God is our Father. No politician can protect you like your father. Many Christians have decided they need a nation in support of religious liberty to preserve and protect the faith. But history has shown us that the more Christians depend on the state to protect the faith, the more the faith crumbles.

Christianity has flourished under persecution. When Christians fixate on political protections, they turn to idol worship and lose their way. This is not to say that Christians should seek out persecution. I'm also not saying that Christians should not participate, as Americans, in the political process. But when our priorities become too political, we look to idols like Supreme Court majorities and strong presidents to save us.

---

[141] John Calvin, *Institutes of Christian Religion*, I.II.8 (United Kingdom: Hendrickson Publishers, 2008), p. 55.

What do we need with these idols? We have God Himself, who is our Father. We may very well experience persecution; Jesus warned us to expect it. But if we do, God will see us through it. Christian, you're a child of the living God. If you aren't acting like it in every aspect of your life, including your politics, have you really embraced the adoption you claim? As Maximus the Confessor said, "A theology without practice is a theology of demons." Practice your theology in every aspect of your life.

My faith has made me committed to protecting and preserving life. My faith has softened my views on immigration. My faith has made me more willing to speak up against the encroaching Gnosticism when others cannot or do not. My faith leads me to reject tribalism and the temptation to turn a blind eye when our side does something wrong.

Faith cannot be silent, and it should shape our politics without politics shaping our faith. For that to be so, we need to be plugged into a healthy church community.

The Danger of Isolation

Even before the pandemic, the trend in our country has been away from participation in a local church. Since 1937, when Gallup first started measuring church attendance, the percentage of Americans who are members of a church, synagogue, or mosque has dropped from 73 percent to 47 percent in 2020. The sharpest decline has been in the past decade.[142] And it's not just our church community connections that are declining.

---

[142] Jeffrey M. Jones, "U.S. Church Membership Falls Below Majority for First Time," Gallup, March 29, 2021, https://news.gallup.com/poll/341963/church-membership-falls-below-majority-first-time.aspx.

We know fewer people personally. We connect to people online. We live in an age of isolation. We don't have to know our immediate neighbors. We construct communities of like-minded people on social media whom we don't really know. We become "friends" with people on Instagram and obsess over their lives. But all we know about them is what they show us on social media.

We've created an illusion in our heads by assuming that our online friends are just like us. When it turns out that they have views diametrically opposed to ours, we turn against them for betraying our image of them. Celebrity culture, even in the church, follows the same cycle.

How many people follow celebrity pastors and theologians and trust them more than their local pastors? With sermons, podcasts, and full church services online, we can "join" a church across the country every week instead of going to church in person.

No need to worry about disagreements within the local church body over politics or style of worship. Just search until you find a pastor or church online that aligns with your preferences. You don't even have to get dressed and talk to people in person. And when the celebrity pastor says something offensive to you? You just move on to the next one.

Isolation is one of the major problems in our culture we aren't discussing enough. Isolation has a myriad of health effects including increased anxiety. The pandemic obviously made it worse, but the problem was there before the virus.

We live busy lives with full schedules and often want to be left alone at the end of the day. If you're an introvert like me, you completely understand this. However, if you isolate yourself from friends and community, you don't feel rested and calm. Studies show that anxiety only increases.

The crisis of isolation is especially affecting men. Most men are living in social isolation. One writer called it a friendship recession. A study by the Survey Center on American Life found that only 27 percent of men have at least six close friends, down from 55 percent in 1990. Twenty percent of single men said they don't have any close friends.[143]

As an introvert, being around lots of people makes me anxious. I'm connected to more and more people in my life on a social basis but fewer and fewer are close friends with whom I want to hang out and have deep, meaningful conversations.

What I'm finding, and what these studies are showing, is that many men have regular contact with a large group of people, but little of it is meaningful or fulfilling. You have lots of people who want to connect on a social level but fewer people you can be vulnerable with. This friendship deficit turns into a mental health issue.

The rise of therapists and psychotherapists is actually not healthy for society. It's one of those reasons why I really (as much as I talk about wanting to keep people at arm's length right now) feel like I need to be intentional about connecting with people for meaningful interaction on a regular basis.

The data is showing that we have a crisis in mental health, particularly for men in this country right now, as they have given up meaningful relationships with a smaller number of people for

---

[143] Daniel Cox, "American Men Suffer a Friendship Recession," *National Review*, July 6, 2021, https://www.nationalreview.com/2021/07/american-men-suffer-a-friendship-recession/.

minimal relationships with a maximum number of people. And do you know what the side point of this is? It corresponds to a decrease in men going to church.

Women in this country continue to go to church. Men in this country do not. Their isolation corresponds to a decrease in engagement in church and civic organizations. The moral of the story is, get yourself involved in a spiritual community and you will be healthier long-term.

The more men are isolated from everyone, including from spiritual activities like a church, the rate of suicide, depression, alcoholism, and drug abuse only increases. If you want to solve those problems, get yourself plugged in.

Connect with the Local Faith Community

Let us consider how to stir up one another
to love and good works, not neglecting
to meet together, as is the habit of some,
but encouraging one another, and all the
more as you see the Day drawing near.
—Hebrews 10:24–25, ESV

Archbishop William Temple famously said, "The Church exists primarily for the sake of those who are still outside it." And to a certain extent, he's right. One of the central purposes of the church is to proclaim the gospel. However, the gospel isn't just for unbelievers. Believers need the church and the gospel the way the wounded need a hospital and medical care. We come to church to worship God and to be refreshed and restored. It's essential to find a solid church to belong to.

During the height of the pandemic, many places of worship moved their services online to protect the medically vulnerable in their congregations and communities. It was wise and necessary at the time, but it created challenges for churches as they sought to provide physical and spiritual care. People needed to know whether the church doors were open or not; people of faith do not close up shop.

Some churches, mosques, temples, and synagogues responded by stepping into the breach of fear and going toward the illness, not away from it. Volunteers provided meals and checked on those who were sick. As the months dragged on, some churches expanded their outreach to cover the financial needs of their congregations.

Many also reached out to their local community and provided for those in need while helping local nonprofits to help others. The pandemic gave us opportunities to demonstrate what loving your neighbors is all about. Church community should be so much more than an hour on Saturday or Sunday. It is about seeking the welfare of your neighbors—the saved and the lost, the believer and the unbeliever.

Sadly, the pandemic did not bring out the best in all churches and congregations. Some participated in the politicization of the crisis and contributed to the polarization of the political parties. At a time of growing antagonism toward people of faith in this country, some churches and believers put party politics over caring for people in need, which drove more people away from church. Some people left churches because they disagreed with mask and vaccine decisions—either for or against. Others got used to watching church online and don't want to come back.

The thing is, we were created for community. God didn't give Adam a smartphone or computer to have someone to talk to or sermons to listen to. Instead, God made Eve because it wasn't good for Adam to be alone. God walked in the garden with Adam and Eve. He didn't just yell down from heaven or leave them on their own to figure things out.

We need to be in a physical community, not just a digital one. The tendency with digital communities is to surround ourselves with people who look, sound, and think like us. That way we are never exposed to diverse opinions or have to deal with people who disagree with us. Physical community is good for our souls. It strengthens us and improves our interpersonal skills.

As we see in the Hebrews passage quoted above, the Bible tells us we need to worship with other people. We need to gather so we can encourage each other. We need to conform our thoughts, ideas, and worldview to biblical teaching. We need the community of other believers in worship, and we can't do it alone or exclusively online.

How can we find a good church? Many churches claim to be missional by focusing all their efforts on converting unbelievers. But a truly missional church is one that brings in believers, disciples them, and equips them to go out and share the gospel with unbelievers.

In a healthy church, the sermons are focused on equipping believers as the pastor works his way through the Bible in a thoughtful and purposeful way. When the preacher isn't preaching on a hot button issue every week, or speaking as if giving a TED Talk, those are signs of a good church.

A church should be welcoming to all strangers, whether believers or not. You need a church where you are part of a community, where the people in your church know your name and care for you. Many megachurches out there are designed for multitudes of people, but it's easy to get lost in the crowd and have no real connection or community. If you don't have connection or community in church, find a local church where you fit in and can be involved.

We also need to read Scripture, and not selectively. Read through the Bible. Don't go find the passage that sparks the mood of the day. Read Scripture systematically. Once you've read a passage, chapter, or book, then read what other people have written about it. You might also read a daily devotional.

Don't read politics into Scripture. Read Scripture into politics. Too many people on the Left and the Right conform their religion to their politics instead of their politics to their religion. My rule of thumb is if the Bible never challenges what you believe about the world and politics, you're probably reading the Bible with the wrong intentions. The Bible should challenge all of us about what we think and believe.

I have long been critical of the liberal image of weepy, huggy Jesus who emphasizes only compassion and acceptance. Too often this view of Jesus is an idol made in liberals' own image. I'm increasingly concerned that conservative Christians are making an idol out of a masculine, wrathful image of Jesus.

Christianity cannot be a masculine Christianity of gym bro jackasses giving the Left swirlies. Instead, we need to focus on taking responsibility for our families and raising a future generation to love the Lord. There's a quiet strength in humble living.

Some on the Right believe we have to save our country to share the gospel. They are afraid Christians will be silenced for their faith unless they stand and defend the United States and the First Amendment. They believe they must fight for America to advance Christ's mission as the shining city on a hill.

But it's a patriot's gospel, not the gospel of Jesus. No country on Earth is eternal or pre-eminent. Christians, we share the gospel to save souls for God. Our mission is not to go forth and preach, teach, and baptize so we can save the United States. We preach, teach, and baptize in the name of the Father, Son, and Holy Spirit to make disciples of all peoples for the Kingdom of God.

Many Christians have made an idol of the nation. To advance the gospel, some think they have to fight for the nation. But Americans are not God's chosen people. You are chosen if you believe in Christ. The early Christians were persecuted relentlessly. They face death everywhere they turned, and still they shared the gospel.

Like them, you do not need social media or even religious freedom to share the gospel. Christians in America have a stewardship obligation to participate in the political process. But do not be so committed to your nation that you are less committed to Christ. Christ must be first and foremost. Christianity is the only religion not tied to a geographic location. Long after the United States is gone, Christ will remain.

For now, this must be said—if you tie the fate of the nation to the advancement of the gospel, you are dabbling in a false gospel. You will not save this nation. It does not mean you should abandon it or fail to be a good steward of it. But Christ is King, the gates of hell will not stand against Him, and He will prevail with or without a United States of America.

Jesus is going to come back and sort everything out for us. We don't have to worry. In the meantime, you've got to love your neighbor as yourself, do unto others as you want them to do unto you, and seek the welfare of your local community while praying for it and your civic leaders. Above all else, remember all things really do work for the good of those called according to His purpose.

Unplug and Focus

"Eighty and six years I have served Him, and He has done me no wrong," said Polycarp, bishop of Smyrna, in 156, A.D., before climbing onto a pyre where Roman authorities would burn him to death. Eyewitnesses reported the local authorities respected Polycarp and begged him to recant his faith in Christ. He would not. The Romans did not even tie Polycarp to a post because they knew he would not flee the fire. Polycarp fed his captors, prayed over them, then climbed the pyre to die.

Authorities carted off Polycarp's friend Ignatius, bishop of Antioch, and fed him to wild beasts in the Circus Maximus on July 6, 108. Ignatius also refused to renounce Christ. Histories of the time, their personal writings, and the writings of others tell us that Polycarp and Ignatius were students of the Apostle John. They vouched for him as the author of his gospel. John installed Polycarp as bishop of Smyrna, and the Apostle Peter placed Ignatius in charge of Antioch.

In 99, A.D., the Romans drowned Clement in the sea tied to an anchor for the same reason. Paul mentioned Clement in his letter to the Philippians, and history shows Clement interacted with Peter, Paul, and John.

Clement, Ignatius, and Polycarp were one generation removed from the direct eyewitnesses of Jesus. They were students of the Apostles. They vouched for the veracity of the letters forming the New Testament. They died refusing to reject Jesus as the Christ.

Some skeptics say Jesus did not exist, but by any historic standard, the man known as Jesus of Nazareth existed. If He did not exist, then neither did the Greek philosopher Socrates. We have no writings from Socrates himself. We only know of him through the writings of other people. But no one doubts that Socrates existed.

We actually have more eyewitness accounts of Jesus's existence than of Socrates'. Some, however, argue that because Jesus made claims of divinity, there must be extraordinary evidence. Perhaps of His divinity, but not for His existence.

The Apostle John was Jesus's best friend. We know this from Scripture. We also know this from Polycarp, Ignatius, and others. They studied under John, recounted his stories of being with Jesus, including stories not in Scripture, and confirmed John, Peter, Paul and others as eyewitnesses to Christ's Resurrection.

According to John, Jesus's own brothers rejected His claims of divinity. At Jesus's death, John had to care for Mary because none of Jesus's brothers or sisters went with Mary to the crucifixion. John, Luke, Paul, and others tell us Jesus's brothers later became leaders in the early Christian church.

Histories of the era recount that James and Jude, Jesus's brothers, wrote the New Testament letters named after them. Both were executed for proclaiming Jesus as the risen Lord. In fact, the Romans ultimately exterminated the entirety of Jesus's earthly family.

The leaders of Jerusalem respected James. The oral and written histories of the early Christian church recount that they asked James to publicly deny claims of Jesus's divinity. Instead, James proclaimed his brother Jesus, whom he had originally rejected, was God. The leaders of the city, enraged, carried James to the top of the temple wall in Jerusalem and threw him off to his death.

Jesus could have been a conman surrounded by other conmen. But would conmen be willing to die to keep the con going? Or, there is something else. Dozens have claimed to be the Christ, but only Jesus is remembered and worshiped as the Christ. Why? Perhaps because it is true.

Occasionally I am asked if I really believe that faith in Jesus Christ is necessary to get into heaven. Yes, I really believe that. I don't want a religion in which everyone goes to heaven no matter what. The whole idea of universalism, meaning that everyone gets into heaven, is anathema to the idea of justice. There are awful people who do awful things, and I believe God is just. Sharing eternity with unrepentant monsters would not be just.

But what about all the good people? Show me a saint, and I'll show you someone who sinned. We all sin. As Scripture tells us, we all fall short. None of us deserves eternity. It is only by God's grace, and our faith in Him that we obtain it.

Why Jesus then? Why is Christianity the only exclusive path to salvation? This is a matter of faith. As much as a Muslim believes that Islam is the only way to eternity, I believe in Christianity. It is not a blind faith. Unlike other religions where the founders witnessed private events and private miracles and became designated prophets who could change things up until their death, Christianity is a religion built on a public ministry and public miracles of a man not claiming to be a prophet, but God Himself.

We have the eyewitness testimony of Matthew, John, Paul, James, Jude, Peter, Mark, and Luke, of the eyewitnesses Luke interviewed, of the students of John, Paul, and Peter, and of others. We have an eyewitness-written record going back to only a few decades after Christ's Resurrection.

We have the written works of the Apostle John's students recounting the things that John taught them. We have more than 5,000 copies of manuscripts written within a few hundred years of the Resurrection. No other religion has the copious, written documentation compiled within such a short period of time, save for the Judaism on which Christianity is premised.

Buddhism, Islam, and Judaism all have geographic anchors. Christianity is a global religion of enormous consequence free from the shackles of a geographic capital. Even most secular histories put Jesus's crucifixion on the top ten list of most important moments in human history.

Ultimately, I do believe by faith. I believe because I see the interactions of a living God in my life. My faith sustained me when my wife was misdiagnosed and given six months to live, sustained me as I lay in a hospital bed on the verge of death, and continues to sustain me as my wife now battles her cancer. Yes, I really do believe these things and am not ashamed of them.

Jesus is the living God—Yahweh incarnate. I'm blessed with a platform where I can share the good news. Perhaps cancel culture can shut me down but cancel culture cannot cancel the cross.

Remember: God Is Sovereign

In my work, I encounter many atheists. Some are very hostile. Some are curious. Almost all of them seem to think it is far easier for a Christian to rely on his "imaginary sky god" than accept the fatal existence of humanity. I beg to differ.

It seems far easier for a person to conclude there is no God in heaven and no divine sovereignty so everything that happens is just some random act. It is far easier to be an atheist than a Christian.

A Christian must contend with the sovereignty of God. When a Christian works for something, prays about it, and it doesn't happen, he will wonder why and wonder what God's plan must be. When an atheist works for something, he has no god to pray to, and failure or success comes entirely through his own efforts or lack thereof. There is no God.

Without God, there is no wondering, no guessing, no praying, and no second-guessing like Christians do if God doesn't answer their prayers or deliver the result they want. There's no crying out to God in disappointment. There's no praising God with excitement. There's just nothing.

The older Christians get, the more they have to come to terms with God's sovereignty and control. They gain understanding that a person's hard work and God go hand in hand. While we might see either only God at work or only man at work, a complete picture incorporates the sovereignty of God working *with* us. We eventually find peace in God's plan for us.

Do atheists worry about these things? They cannot find comfort in God's sovereignty like a Christian can. The thing you prayed for and did not get is part of His sovereign will for your good. Often it means He has something better in store for you. And sometimes, through the fretting and struggling, Christians end up with their heart's desire and a newer, deeper appreciation for God's role in their lives.

An atheist looks at the evil, savagery, and random violence of the world and wonders why. A Christian not only looks upon it and understands sin but is interrogated by atheists to justify belief in a God who would allow it to happen.

But a Christian has answers while an atheist has none. It is sometimes hard to be a Christian. It is also a reminder that we are passing through this world headed to greater glory. We just have to remember that God's got this, even when it seems like He doesn't. God is sovereign, and the struggle, the success, and the disappointment all pull us closer to trusting in Him.

When we stand before God on the Day of Judgment, He's not going to ask us who we voted for. He's going to ask how we advanced His kingdom. I fear too many Christians are losing sight of this and are trying to advance politicians and political agendas instead.

Do not tie Christ to a party. Do not bear your cross in the name of a politician. Show grace. Love your neighbor. Remember this, too, is fleeting. Above all else, do not be discouraged.

Be in the town square and in politics. But be in both to glorify God, not to advance sinners and their agendas. Be willing to be at odds with those around you for God cares not a bit about your political agenda. He cares that you glorify Him. Whether sharing the burden of cancer or the burden of the church or the burden of culture, God's got this.

All things work for His glory. Be encouraged. Do not be afraid. You worship a God who holds the universe in the palms of His hands.

Here's my challenge for you: Go break bread with someone this week.

CHAPTER 10

SEEK THE WELFARE OF
YOUR COMMUNITY

*Where, then, did the moral values of Western,
liberal, secular culture come from, including
the importance of the individual, equality,
rights, love, and concern for the poor, and
the necessity of improving material conditions for everyone? Many scholars have made
a strong historical case that they came down
to us from Jewish and Christian thought.*
—Timothy Keller

Do you remember where you were on September 11, 2001?
Many of us were glued to the news, watching in shocked hor-
ror as the events unfolded. Others spent hours trying to contact
friends and family to make sure they were OK. The images are
seared in our memories. As New York Governor George Pataki

said, "On that terrible day, a nation became a neighborhood, all Americans became New Yorkers."[144]

And we really did. We were united by our shared grief and our work to repair and restore our nation. Those weren't just empty words. Thousands of people from around the country made their way to New York to help with the recovery efforts. Firefighters and ironworkers cleared away debris, searched for survivors, and recovered the dead. Restaurants brought meals to the workers. Religious leaders from all backgrounds prayed with and for the volunteers. People who couldn't travel to New York donated needed supplies.

On the days following September 11, 2001, we were one people. Race and ethnicity did not matter. Young people signed up to protect and defend the nation. People, as Americans, went to church together, comforted each other, prayed together, and cared for each other. We flew the American flag proudly. And we promised to never forget. As President George W. Bush said at the dedication of the Pentagon memorial: "One of the worst days in America's history saw some of the bravest acts in Americans' history. We'll always honor the heroes of 9/11. And here at this hallowed place, we pledge that we will never forget their sacrifice."[145]

But we have forgotten. We've forgotten the sacrifices. We've forgotten our unity. Two decades later, Americans are rioting in

---

[144] George Pataki, "Text of Gov. Pataki's RNC Speech," CBS News, September 2, 2004, https://www.cbsnews.com/news/text-of-gov-patakis-rnc-speech/.

[145] George W. Bush, "President George W. Bush Speaking at the Dedication of the Pentagon Memorial," U.S. Army, September 11, 2008, https://www.army.mil/article/12325/president_george_w_bush_speaking_at_the_dedication_of_the_pentagon_memorial_sept_11_2008.

the streets, burning down buildings, bashing in the doors at the Capitol, and treating each other as the enemy. Academics have reimagined 9/11 as an attack on the "heteropatriarchy" of the United States. Kids are taught in school that the United States is an oppressive bastion of white privilege where only white people can achieve the American dream, whatever it actually means to people these days. We have turned inward and against each other, and politicians egg us on. We have forgotten. But it's not too late to remember what should unite us.

The Common Good

A growing number of people on the Right are embracing something they're calling Common Good Conservatism. Essentially this means using government as the Left does. As the argument goes, the Left is forcing businesses and using mob tactics to take action against conservatives. Why can't conservatives use the mob or the government to force progressives to do things?

For example, the Left wants to force a baker to bake a cake. Jack Phillips, the baker in Colorado, is being sued for the fifth time. So why can't conservatives use the government to level the playing field? Many of these people want to harness government power to enact conservative policy. They want to embrace big-government conservatism and force corporations to enact a conservative agenda just like the Left does.

Forget about limited government. Forget about restraining the government. Let's do to them what they do to us. We'll use government against them as they use government against us. Sounds alluring, doesn't it?

There are two major flaws with Common Good Conservatism. First, I don't know if you know this, but Republican candidates have not won the popular vote in a presidential election since 2004. Bush versus Kerry was the last time Republicans won the popular vote even though they were able to win the electoral college in 2016.

Since 1988, there's only been one national election where Republicans won the popular vote. If you want the government to impose morality, at some point you have to recognize there are more voters on their side than on ours. How can we convince them to join our side? It won't be by getting even and retaliating. We've got to change hearts and minds if we want to change the culture.

Second, who determines the meaning of common good? I assure you it's not going to be you and me. It's not going to be the average blue-collar worker or rural family. It's going to be the same elites running the news media and the seats of power in Washington. The morality of Harvard, Yale, and Princeton will continue to govern because that's where the conservative elite come from as well.

This kind of conservatism isn't really conservative, nor is it concerned with the common good. Ultimately, we need some level of morality. It comes from us seeking the welfare of the cities in which we live, as the Bible says, as opposed to imposing our will on everyone through Washington, D.C.

What we need in this country is a real appreciation of federalism in ways neither side possesses. There is a faction on the Right that wants to control Washington and impose conservative values on the country. This faction believes that conservatives have caved while the Left has imposed its values on everyone unhindered. But such retaliation is not the way forward.

What we should be striving for is radical federalism. If California wants to have abortions, gay marriage, and drag queen story hour, let it. If Georgia wants not to have abortions, gay marriage, and drag queen story hour, let it. Let California be California, let Georgia be Georgia. At an activist level, both sides feel compelled to impose their will on other people in this country right now, while the overwhelming majority of the people in this country just want to be left alone.

Middle Georgia, where I live, is fairly pro-life. The state of Georgia should be able to pass a law, if the citizens of Georgia agree, saying, "You can't have an abortion in Georgia." If a woman travels to California to have an abortion, Georgia should let her do it without penalizing her or the nonprofit that covers her travel costs.

Someone living in California who is appalled by California's pro-abortion policies should be free to pack up and move somewhere else without penalty. This is the way federalism should work.

I've got to be honest, if the majority of the people in a state want to have drag queen story hours, they should be free to have them without forcing their decisions on everyone else. I don't have to go, and neither do you. And if the majority of people don't think it's appropriate, the state should be able to say, "Nope, sorry. We don't do that here." Ultimately, you should be free to live in an area that reflects your morality.

I would encourage both sides to understand that while you're at loggerheads over issues, Washington should not matter as much as it does to you. Those who divide their time between cable news and social media feel more divided than ever. As discussed, the news media, advertisers, and politicians profit from these feelings of division. But when we step outside of our self-made echo chambers, we find the division isn't so all-consuming. Even the reddest red states have Democratic voters and the bluest blue states have Republican voters.

In New York, over five million people voted for Joe Biden, but over three million voted for Donald Trump. As conservative as Texas is, Biden received 5.2 million votes to Trump's 5.8 million. This whole idea of, "we just need to break apart the country" sounds good to a minority of people who haven't thought it through. It would be a very bloody affair. The Right would have the rural parts of the country and a lot of guns. The Left would have most cities and the supply chains, and it would starve out the Right. It would be a bloody, bloody affair.

People rushed headlong into civil war in the 1860s. They didn't think of the consequences. Up until 2011 or 2012, the majority of people killed in military conflict in this country had died during the civil war. So many people died. Entire families were split up. Is that what you really want? If you think the country is going to break apart, if you're really concerned that we're headed toward a national divorce because everybody hates each other, go out and make your city a better place. Get offline and turn off the TV. Get out of the political fight and get into the culture around you.

The people who are committed to the idea of a national divorce should volunteer at their nearby women's shelter. They need to lend a hand at their local food bank. They need to stand in line at a soup kitchen and serve the homeless, because they've become so fixated on politics and division that they've lost touch with what's happening in the real world of America.

As everyone fixates on Washington and fights over who controls it, we're more likely to have these conversations about whether we should tear apart our country. Maybe instead of rushing headlong into it and trying to stake out your stand, you should be working to keep the country together. How do you keep the country together? Seek the welfare of the city in which you're in exile and pray for it. There you will find your welfare.

Get Involved in Your Community

Jeremiah 29 is one of my favorite passages of Scripture. After the Jewish people went into exile, the prophet Jeremiah sent them a letter. God told His people:

> Build houses and live in them; plant gardens and eat their produce. Take wives and have sons and daughters; take wives for your sons, and give your daughters in marriage, that they may bear sons and daughters; multiply there, and do not decrease. But seek the welfare of the city where I have sent you into exile, and pray to the Lord on its behalf, for in its welfare you will find your welfare. (Jeremiah 29:5–7, ESV)

There is a growing group of conservatives in the United States who have decided that national politics have become too ugly, too compromising, and too unaligned with their values. They aren't willing to compromise to advance a compromised agenda.

Instead, these people are focusing on the welfare of the cities and states in which they live. They prioritize their families' well-being. Washington, they know, is too far removed from their daily lives. In their minds, Republicans and conservative institutions in Washington have made too many compromises to be effective.

At the end of the Bush Administration and beginning of the Obama era, grassroots groups sprang up around the country to help conservatives at the local level. There were training sessions for conservative activists on simple things, such as how to write editorials for local papers. These grassroots groups provided tools for local activists to contact their state legislatures. They explained how to find city council meeting schedules and how to show up to speak on an issue. They encouraged conservative activists to run for their school boards.

As the Tea Party movement grew, conservative organizations focused on fighting Barack Obama and abandoned the grassroots efforts in the states. The Tea Partiers left behind conservatives who had convinced themselves—often accurately—they could not have a meaningful impact in Washington.

After Donald Trump was elected president, many conservative groups focused on protecting the president, maintaining power, and advancing his agenda. Organizations that should have fought massive spending bills looked the other way. As some conservatives retreated from national politics because they could not stomach the character flaws of the president or the direction of the Republican Party, donors and institutions who had once found ways to keep people engaged locally began to direct money elsewhere.

Local media institutions that used to expose government corruption in city halls are going out of business, and these activists could use the help. In Texas, the group Empower Texans is one of the best nationwide at highlighting government abuse and failures. Empower Texans has a statewide network of local activists who are well-trained and highly motivated. Texas, however, is the exception, not the rule.

Conservatives need to reconsider how to engage on the local level with people who are more worried about their children's education than a border wall. Jeremiah's message is still applicable today. We would be better off seeking the welfare of our local communities because we will find our welfare there. As political winds shift in Washington, helping our local communities address school board issues and city hall corruption will become vitally important.

In 1 Thessalonians 5, Paul instructs us to "test everything; hold fast what is good. Abstain from every form of evil." (1 Thes 5:21-22, ESV) Some translations use "examine everything carefully" instead of "test everything." We need to make sure that everything we do is in accord with what Christ would want.

We are called to be like Christ. We are not to hold to a worldly standard of "good" but to a godly standard of good. When Scripture tells us to examine or test everything and hold to what is good, we are to weigh the cries, demands, and outrages of the world and do what Scripture instructs. We are to abstain from evil, despite what the world wants us to do.

Frequently in politics, in culture, and in shaping public policy, Christians are called to respond to an injustice in the world. But the world that caused the injustice in the first place demands a solution that goes against Scripture.

Christians need to stand up and be bold against injustice as we always have been. Christians led the abolitionist movement against slavery. Today, we must lead the movement against the racism in our society. But we have to fight armed with Scripture and Christ, not with worldliness. We must commit ourselves to follow Scripture, and we must work to make this world better. We must abstain from evil and not compromise in favor of so-called lesser evils. We cannot right old wrongs with new ones.

Much of the rage of the world focuses less on justice and injustice, and more on power and lack of power. Too often, injustice means the party out of power wants power, and justice is when it gets power. But we must examine everything and hold fast to what is good. And what is good?

It is good to seek the equality of all people before the law, to help the widows, the poor, the orphans, and the refugees. It is good to love your neighbor as yourself and do good to others. It is good to remember this world and this nation are temporary, and that we are headed to eternity. It is good to remember we do not need politics and government to save us. We have Jesus.

None of us has been to heaven, but we have seen, by faith, a glimpse of it in the Resurrection. This is where we place our hope and trust. We should live in this hope and know we have seen eternity. We should bring that to the world because we have examined it and we know it is good. We know it will last when all around us crumbles.

Invest Locally

Conservatives can try and sometimes succeed at winning nationally. But locally, there's a whole lot that can happen if we just spend some time. Years ago, I was elected to my city council. The only reason I ran was because I noticed the proliferation of Asian-themed massage parlors in my town. As I did some research, I found ties to human trafficking. I felt emboldened to run for office and to shut them down.

If we believe in Scripture, we should expect things to get worse in this country for people of faith. When the persecution heats up, we can't expect Washington to save us, or really care what happens to us. It's not that Washington and national politics are unimportant. But when we spend so much time focusing on Washington, we forget we have a ministry field in our backyard.

As we've seen, Scripture exhorts us to take care of our local community, not just our nation. We need to plant roots in our local communities, know our neighbors, and help them as good neighbors. If we all started investing ourselves in our local communities, we'd see improvements. And with local improvements, we'd improve our states overall. And by improving each state, we'd improve the nation. The roots of our nation matter.

As a society, we get stuck inside our tribal comfort zones. Much of the press leans Left and so adds to tribal thinking. Also, politicians from both sides feed off grievances for power. Neither side has any incentive to find a solution when both profit by keeping the discord going, as we've discussed.

Americans would be better off abandoning the quaint—and repeatedly proven false notion—of Washington having the solution for what ails us. As President Reagan famously said, "The nine most terrifying words in the English language are, 'I'm from the government, and I'm here to help.'"[146] Washington, inevitably,

---

[146] Ronald Reagan, press conference, August 12, 1986.

makes most things worse, especially beyond the core functions of government. Americans are obsessed with Washington, presidential elections, and national political parties.

People think Washington will provide the solutions if they just put up enough black squares on Instagram. But Washington will not provide the solution, and most likely your state capitol will not either. *You* will provide the solution.

If the federal government is the provider and securer of all liberties, then whoever controls it also controls all the power. One side will get the power and refuse to give it up. The best way forward is what the Founders envisioned—spread the power out across the country. Make the state and local governments more powerful.

We need to advance culturally conservative positions locally: end indoctrination of school children with critical race theory, prohibit boys from competing in girls' sports, protect conservatives on college campuses by passing campus free speech laws and using boards of regents to promote ideological and intellectual diversity on college campuses, and advance religious freedom acts in the states without them.

We need to recognize and accept that there will be consequences. It is probably only a matter of time before the Left convinces California to end the tax-exempt status of Christian schools if they do not comply with California indoctrination programs. We have to acknowledge that some states will respond to our actions by going in the opposite direction. And we have to be able to accept it.

Our goal should be to empower people at local levels to live in communities of interest and use the government to prevent corporations and other governments from discriminating against or punishing those local communities where they have opted for morally conservative living. In reality, we need clear guidance from the Supreme Court so that states cannot punish a person or business for exercising their First Amendment right.

Ironically, corporations have a role to play by engaging in interstate business without pressuring states to conform to one ideology or another. So far, they are failing to do so. One approach would be to end corporate welfare of all kinds, including tax, legislative, and regulatory perks that allow big corporations to insulate themselves against the market forces and the consequences of their political stances.

Some conservatives have funded private schools in the country so they can open their doors to poor kids in failing public schools. The minds being wasted in the indoctrination of many failing public schools could be harnessed in settings like that. It seems a multimillion-dollar campaign to fund scholarships for kids into Christian schools would be a better use of the money than another research study on public policy.

If we stop pouring so much money into conservative Washington think tanks, we will have more funds to set up freely accessible private schools for the poor in urban areas. Parents are more concerned about indoctrination than the latest think tank white paper. If we can help to get children out of government schools, we'll reduce the need for government schools.

Seek the welfare of your city and there, not Washington, will you find your welfare. If you can give time and labor, do so. If you can't, give money. If you can't, give prayer and moral support. Give to the *local* food bank, the *local* soup kitchen, the *local* homeless shelter, the *local* domestic violence clinic, the *local* schools—give, work, pray, and invest in *your* city. You, not politicians or political parties, can fix this.

Grassroots Cultural Change

As discussed, a growing strain of American Christians want to use the government to advance Christian values in the country. There's nothing wrong with that, but the way to do it is through electing Christians who use their moral values to shape their votes and public policy. This is how our country was designed to work and how it has always worked. People win elections and use their positions to advance causes they believe in.

Unfortunately, some on the Right are promoting increasingly authoritarian methods. They model themselves after autocratic leaders in Europe and Asia. Their policies and plans hinge on gaining power and never losing it, whatever it takes. American Christians should resist this.

Foolishly, some Christians with online platforms are embracing labels like "Christian nationalist," which adds fodder to the Leftist goal of smearing the entire concept of Christian liberty in America. The religious Left hates orthodox Christianity, and the Left-leaning press doesn't know the difference between mainline and conservative denominations. They have no incentive to differentiate between the authoritarian and "Christian nationalist" extremes and the majority of Christians who have no interest in either. The political Left is capitalizing on this opportunity to tie all Christians in America to these ideas.

The Left has made private corporations agents of imposing its will. The conservative response shouldn't be to increase government oversight and regulation. That only plays into the Left's hand. The methods we use can and will be used against us. Instead, our response should be conservative grassroots organization.

From groups like The Heritage Foundation, Americans for Tax Reform, the Family Research Council, and the American Family Association to the Media Research Center, R Street, the Conservative Partnership, and the Club for Growth, we need to figure out ways to coordinate local efforts aimed at limiting private corporations doing the Left's bidding.

The problem is that the national conservative movement is largely broken. Too many grifters have invaded the movement, and too many conservative organizations are beholden to large corporations. Likewise, too many supposedly principled organizations are bent on shaping the movement according to Trump's will, and a vocal group of conservatives is ready to burn the country down in response to the Left.

I'm not sure if unity can be found at the national level. But we should try. The Left is able to influence culture right now in large part because of the disarray and disunity of the Right. At the local level, we can unite around the economic clout of churchgoers, conservatives, and Republican voters.

Though culture may be upstream from politics, we need to remember that spirit is upstream from culture. Evangelical churches need to be involved in this process too. Solid, sensible policy needs to be deployed. If we're just "owning the Left," the Left will beat us every time.

We need to respond to these challenges and misrepresentations, but how? Right now, we need to take a united stand.

Christians active at the local level is the most fruitful response. Feeding the hungry, providing for widows and orphans, educating our future generation, and sharing the gospel with people who wonder why they exist—these are the best uses of the church and its resources in America. This is not an abdication of Christianity in America. It is building a stable generation of Christians in America who'll be ready to take the leadership reins of the nation.

Several times in the New Testament, the Apostle Paul tells Christians to seek a quiet life. American Christians have had the comfort of a society that largely has agreed with them for a long time. But those times are fading away and old hostilities against Christians have started trickling back into the national dialog.

The early Christian church did not stand in the town square to demand its right to be heard. Americans have that privilege. But we should remember the early Christians put their local communities ahead of national conversations and cared for the voiceless and powerless around them. They converted an empire with care, not demands.

Politics Won't Save Us, But Jesus Will

I'm a Christian, first and foremost. As a Christian, I know we are all sinners. Because I know we are all sinners, I am a conservative who wants to limit the power of the sinners in charge of our government. We should have a free marketplace of ideas. We should embrace negative liberties (we can do things on our own) and reject positive liberties (the government must provide for us). Conservatism has traditionally supported individuals and families without government interference.

For a long time in the United States, both liberals and conservatives embraced the idea of liberty while arguing over the role of the government. The Left has worked toward a greater social safety net, while the Right has promoted greater freedoms for people to both succeed and fail. We have argued, but the arguments have had a shared moral underpinning.

Now, it seems we are a people with many different moral foundations arguing not about how to take the next step forward, but about which direction we should go. We are in the middle of a political realignment.

We live in a postmodern era. In postmodernity, there is no objective truth. Reality is shaped by words and belief. And devotion to a belief requires public performance. Postmodernism is arguably incompatible with the American nation founded on self-evident, objective truths.

And so we see boisterous performances on the Left and the Right. The Left engages in protests, cancel culture, and demands for censorship. The Right engages in protests, cancel culture, and demands for censorship. Everyone wants to be free to act largely devoid of ideas or truth, while driven by contempt for the other side.

Joseph Henrich, an atheist, wrote a book, *The WEIRDest People in the World: How the West Became Psychologically Peculiar and Particularly Prosperous*. WEIRD is an acronym for "Western, educated, industrialized, rich, and democratic." The book is about how Christianity provided a level of civilization that moved Westerners away from tribalism and into democratic society. He also makes a point by stating that as Christianity fades, countries move away from democracy back to authoritarian and tribalism.

When our nation was founded, almost everybody had a belief in God and divine justice, or at least respected the belief. You could be a member of society and love the people you disagreed with, knowing you weren't responsible for meting out justice as an individual. If society didn't take care of justice, God would.

In a post-Christian society, people expect to be judge, jury, and executioner because there is no God Who upholds justice. This leads to cancel culture and civic instability. Even culturally Christian people, who aren't really believers, behave as if they have a role in shaping the future because they are no longer grounded in the idea of God being in control of things.

A great many people on the Right are vying for power now. Many are going to ask Christians to vote for them while jettisoning Christian values behind the scenes. Some will claim to support a Christian worldview or promise to use Christian values to advance the kingdom on Earth. But be careful. Many are willing to lie to, manipulate, and take advantage of Christians on their path to gain and maintain power.

Part of the angst of the present age is the spiritual collapse going on around us. People look to strong leaders and rally to causes promising to protect us and our way of life. Many such causes mean well, but none of them will succeed. As Scripture says: "For here we have no lasting city, but we seek the city that is to come. Through him then let us continually offer up a sacrifice of praise to God, that is, the fruit of lips that acknowledge his name. Do not neglect to do good and to share what you have, for such sacrifices are pleasing to God." (Hebrews 13:14–16, ESV)

As Christians, we do not fight as the world does. Our fight is not against flesh and blood, but against the spiritual forces of evil. God arms us with His strength. He is the One who saves us from our enemies. We can be strong and courageous and not terrified or discouraged, for the Lord our God will be with us wherever we go. We do not need to be afraid for the Lord Himself will fight for us.

Don't lose your hope in Christ as you engage in politics. No politician, no party, no platform, no policy, and no idea will save you from the world. The world will steadily advance with all its paganism and Gnosticism until Christ Himself returns. Don't sell your soul for a Pyrrhic victory. For all the bluster and promises, politics can't save you.

We need to be discerning and stop trying to find political protection from spiritual warfare. Conservatives have been trying to fight spiritual battles with political weapons. It will not work. Remember, Christians must live and work and engage with politics differently from the world. The world will likely consider you weak. But God sees and knows, and what is weakness to the world is strength in the Lord.

Seek the welfare of your city and pray for it. Somewhere in your local community, there is a homeless person who needs help. Somewhere, right now, a husband is hitting his wife, and she's about to pack up their children and escape to a women's shelter. Tonight, a family is going to lose their home in a fire and have nowhere to turn. A family whose jobs disappeared with the pandemic will need help from the local food bank. A child will slip further behind in literacy at a local school. An elderly couple will go another day without contact with other people.

Whoever is president and whichever party controls the Senate or your state legislature will be unable to fix those things.

They will have zero impact in any meaningful way on the lives of those people. But you can.

We have all obsessed over national elections and politics. We all have an interest in it. But the homeless, the abused wife and child, the hungry, and the isolated are not relying on a president, a senator, or a congressman. They need your commitment to your local community. They need a neighbor's love.

When Scripture says to seek the welfare of the city in which you live, you can do it by voting, but elections only come on one day every other year. Every day of the year, someone in your community is in need. You are better able to serve that person than is anyone in Washington.

We need to remember that politics should not be all-encompassing in our lives. Both sides will try to convince you that if their guy loses, the country is going to hell in a handbasket. I assure you, despite the hysteria, it's not likely. But right now someone in your community is falling through the cracks, and you can help.

Let us not grow weary of doing good, for in due season we will reap, if we do not give up. The Lord is our strength, our rock, our fortress, our deliverer, our shield, and our stronghold. No weapon forged against us will prosper, and we will refute every tongue that accuses us—this is the heritage of the Lord's servants. For the battle is the Lord's.

Therefore, put on the full armor of God so when the day of evil comes, we may be able to stand our ground. In all these things we are more than conquerors through Him who loves us. And we know God causes everything to work together for the good of those who love God and are called according to His purpose. Seek the welfare of your community and please go love your neighbor today, tomorrow, and the day after that.

CHAPTER 11

LET GO OF WORRY AND ANXIETY

Worrying is carrying tomorrow's load with
today's strength—carrying two days at once.
It is moving into tomorrow ahead of time.
Worrying doesn't empty tomorrow of its
sorrow, it empties today of its strength.
—Corrie Ten Boom

The night of the Last Supper, Jesus washed His disciples' feet and told them that one of them was going to betray Him. After Judas, the betrayer, had gone, Jesus told the remaining disciples that He would be leaving them for a while. He was talking about His death and Resurrection, but the disciples didn't understand at the time. They were understandably worried. Where was Jesus going? Why couldn't they go with Him?

To comfort and reassure them, Jesus said: "Let not your hearts be troubled. Believe in God; believe also in me. In my Father's house are many rooms. If it were not so, would I have told you that

I go to prepare a place for you? And if I go and prepare a place for you, I will come again and will take you to myself, that where I am you may be also." (John 14:1–3, ESV) Jesus told the disciples not to worry or be anxious because He was going to prepare a place for them and He would return. He also told them that He would send the Holy Spirit to help and comfort them. He warned them that the world would hate them, like it hated Him. But for every warning about the hard things they would face, Jesus encouraged them that they were not alone and didn't need to fear: "Peace I leave with you; my peace I give to you. Not as the world gives do I give to you. Let not your hearts be troubled, neither let them be afraid.... I have said these things to you, that in me you may have peace. In the world you will have tribulation. But take heart; I have overcome the world." (John 14:27, 16:33, ESV)

The peace Jesus promised isn't like the false promises the world gives. It's real, lasting, and eternal. It's grounded in God's promises, and He is always faithful to His word. Jesus told the disciples that life would be hard, but He promised that even in the hard times, He would be with them. And eventually, they would be with Him forever.

From Matthew's Gospel, we have a list of the twelve Apostles: Simon Peter, Andrew, James the son of Zebedee, John, Philip, Bartholomew, Thomas, Matthew, James the son of Alphaeus, Thaddaeus, Simon the Zealot, and Judas Iscariot (Matthew 10:2–4). After Judas betrayed Jesus and later died, the remaining disciples chose Matthias to replace him (Acts 1:21–26). Along with many other disciples and Christians in the early church, they followed the Great Commission, going to the nations, preaching the gospel, making disciples, baptizing converts, and teaching them how to live as believers. The gospel spread quickly to the corners of the known world. And as Jesus had warned them, the early church faced persecution, and many were martyred.

James the son of Zebedee, was executed by Herod, as recorded in Acts 12:2. Early histories tell us about how the rest of the twelve died. Peter was arrested and killed after Emperor Nero blamed the fire of Rome on Christians. Andrew was crucified in Greece. Philip was arrested and killed by a Roman proconsul. Bartholomew was martyred in Armenia or India. Thomas was killed by soldiers in India. Reports about Matthew's death differ. Some say he was killed in Ethiopia. James the son of Alphaeus, Thaddaeus, Simon the Zealot, and Matthias were all martyred.

Only one of the twelve Apostles died of old age. John was sent to the island of Patmos when Emperor Domitian was persecuting the church. He died there in exile. After Domitian, Emperors Trajan, Hadrian, Decius, Valerian, and Diocletian persecuted Christians in the early church. Arab Muslims discriminated against and martyred Christians living in areas they conquered during the Middle Ages.

During the Protestant Reformation and Counter-Reformation, Protestant and Catholic rulers took turns persecuting Christians on both sides of that divide. As we discussed earlier, many Christians were imprisoned and executed during the French Revolution. The Boxer Rebellion in China led to the deaths of foreign missionaries and Chinese Christians. As Communism took over countries around the world, millions of Christians were persecuted for their faith.

The organization Open Doors ranks the top fifty countries where Christians face the most persecution. As of 2023, the top ten were North Korea, Somalia, Yemen, Eritrea, Libya, Nigeria, Pakistan, Iran, Afghanistan, and Sudan.[147] Christians have always faced persecution.

Through imprisonments, beatings, loss of family and friends, and even to their deaths, Christians around the world and through history have trusted Jesus's promise never to leave them or forsake them. That promise wasn't just for martyrs. It's for all of us who have put our faith in Jesus. He has gone before us, but He has not left us orphans. He's given us the Holy Spirit, and He will come back for us. For that reason, no matter what happens in politics or in our nation or in the world, we can let go of our worry and anxiety and have peace.

Anxiety and Fear Around Us

If you can keep your head when all about you
Are losing theirs and blaming it on you
—Rudyard Kipling

The world seems to have gone nuts. People are seeing unidentified flying objects (UFOs). The government confirms it. Florida Senator Marco Rubio claims that UFOs are flying over our military installations. Pilots have videos of mysterious objects flying rapidly and making ninety-degree turns—something physically impossible for humans at the speed at which those objects are flying. They seem to defy the known laws of physics.

---

[147] Open Doors, "World Watch List 2023," https://www.opendoors.org/en-US/persecution/countries/.

Americans watched other Americans burn down cities while reporters stood in front of the burning rubble claiming that the protests were peaceful, but your eyes might be racist. Supporters of President Trump stormed the United States Capitol; some even erected a gallows with noose to hang the vice president, symbolically or otherwise. Most of the president's supporters, to this day, blame progressives.

The actress Ellen Page has become Elliot Page, following in Bruce Jenner's footsteps. Anyone who points out that men cannot become women is considered a bigot. On university campuses and in Fortune 500 companies across America, "woke" is in, and normal is deviant, bigoted, and shameful. People who speak up about their faith are pilloried and shamed.

The media heralds President Biden as a Christian role model despite his advocacy of abortion and support for policies that would harm Christians, harass nuns, and shut down Christian organizations. Tweets from a decade ago can get a person fired. No apology is enough.

Across the nation, every effort is being made to divide people along racial lines and spark interracial strife. White people are now told they are European Americans and colonizing oppressors. Black people are told they have always been oppressed, and if they deny it, they're told they are feeling the effects of white oppression. Hispanic people are being subdivided into black and white classes. Asian people are punished for their successes, mocked for their family structures, and told they are also oppressed, but also the oppressor.

Children are being indoctrinated in schools. Normalcy is becoming bad, and deviancy must be embraced. Gender dysphoria, once a mental health issue, is now considered mainstream and normal. Gender can change at any time, but a person's sexual orientation is determined at birth.

The world appears to have gone mad.

A lot of you are anxious and want to fight the Left. But, and this is important, we're not going to win this fight. The world hates the things of God. The situation is going to get far worse over time. That doesn't mean we shouldn't speak up and take a stand. But it does mean we should expect to lose more and more.

This is not a call to surrender. It is a call to acknowledge reality. Increasingly, we will see people on the Right become as ruthless as people on the Left. They will fight each other and use each other's tactics in worldly and godless ways. We will see people on the Right attack those of us who stand against their scorched Earth methods. We will see more betrayals from the Right as many embrace the hedonism of the world.

God calls us to love our neighbor. God calls us to turn the other cheek. He calls us to pray for our enemies. He called us to not be like the world, but to glorify God in a fallen world. He never said it would be easy.

There is no reason to fall into despair as the world falls apart, and we see both the Left and the Right revealing themselves as pagans. God calls us to love others and serve Him. The world will seem dominant. The world will look victorious. But in the end, we will win, not because of our arguments, our cunning, or our political strategy. Christians will win because He wins, and we are on His team. So we can be calm even in the midst of the raging storm around us.

When God Seems Silent

How long, O Lord? Will you forget me forever?
How long will you hide your face from me?
—Psalm 13:1, ESV

Sometimes it seems like God isn't listening to our prayers or paying attention to what's going on in our lives or the world around us. Believe me, I understand that. When I feel like God is silent, I find in the Psalms. David, the man after God's own heart, often felt abandoned by God and cried out for God to hear him and help. "How long, O Lord," is a common theme in the Psalms.

In Psalm 90, we read:

> Return, O Lord! How long? Have pity on your servants! Satisfy us in the morning with your steadfast love, that we may rejoice and be glad all our days. Make us glad for as many days as you have afflicted us, and for as many years as we have seen evil. Let your work be shown to your servants, and your glorious power to their children. Let the favor of the Lord our God be upon us, and establish the work of our hands upon us; yes, establish the work of our hands! (Psalm 90:13–17, ESV)

Moses wrote that while wandering in the wilderness after God rescued His people from slavery, Moses saw countless miracles. God met and spoke directly with him, giving him the law and directions for the tabernacle and Ark of the Covenant. The

God of all Creation made His dwelling place with Moses and the Israelites. Yet, Moses feels abandoned, even when he is literally only steps away from the living God.

A pastor friend told me that God is working in your life at this very minute in thousands of different ways, but you may only be aware of three or four of those ways. You may not be aware of any. Just because things don't go the way you want, or in the timeframe you want, does not mean that God is absent or silent.

The week before Christmas 2006, I lost my job on the same day my wife was given six months to live. The doctors told me she had a rare cancer that had spread through her body, into her lungs, and there was no cure. I had to be the one to look my wife in the eye and tell her she was dying.

After I told her, I had to pick up our one-year-old baby from daycare. When we got home, I had no energy left. I just sat in the mud in the rain and cried with our baby patting my face as if to tell me it would be okay.

I didn't really feel like God was around. Everything was not okay.

Once I worked up the energy to get inside and get us cleaned up, all I could do was pray. I found little comfort in the prayers, but I kept praying. At the hospital that night, my wife and I had the conversations no one wants to have.

Late that night, the surgeon who had done the biopsy on my wife's lungs and diagnosed cancer came into the room to tell us that, upon further review, the doctors weren't sure it was cancer and would be conferring with the Mayo Clinic. The Mayo Clinic confirmed that her condition was benign. A few days later, a company in Washington bought my company, and I kept my job.

Over the years, I have prayed earnestly for things for my family, for myself, for my career, and in many of those cases, God never seemed to answer, or at least did not answer on my schedule. But God has always been there. Sometimes I have to remind myself of the times when God has provided, often at the last minute and in unexpected ways. He's been ever present. God has a plan, and it's for our good.

In the spring of 2016, I very publicly said I would not vote for Donald Trump. Men showed up at our house to threaten us. My kids got bullied terribly in school, and the school did nothing. They were literally chased through a store by a man yelling at them that their father was destroying America by not supporting Trump.

I went to the doctor because I was always out of breath. I figured it was allergies, or maybe it was stress. The doctor sent me to the hospital for a CT scan. Next thing I knew they were rushing me into an ICU unit not expecting me to survive the night. My lungs had been filling up with blood clots. My blood oxygen was around 80 percent and falling. The head of the ICU saw my scans and asked if the body had been taken to the morgue. That was me. I spent two weeks in the hospital being treated like I was a stroke victim.

The very same day I was admitted to the ICU, the Mayo Clinic called and said the doctors were pretty sure my wife had lung cancer. Had she not been misdiagnosed a decade before, they would have never caught it until it was too late. Her cancer is rare, genetic, and without a present medical cure. But she takes a pill each day that keeps the tumors from growing. The pill should work for two years. We are past the five-year anniversary.

I am still here. She is still here. God has been very good to us—so good, each time I ask God for something else, I feel a sense of greed thinking He's done enough and maybe I should stop bothering Him. But His mercy is new every morning.

Through it all, I remind myself of all the times God has been there, and also of all the times God seems silent. Even then, He is working in ways I could not imagine at the time—in ways that have provided for me and my family beyond anything I was praying for.

I don't expect the unbeliever to believe. He will see luck, coincidence, or chance. But I know it is the Lord because of that feeling—you who are believers know that feeling and you can't describe it either. It is the feeling I wish the unbeliever could feel, that feeling that Scripture calls the peace that transcends all understanding—that feeling that if they experienced it they'd fall down and worship.

God is not the money bank. He's not a sugar daddy. He's not the genie in the bottle granting wishes. He is the God of all Creation. We are made in His image and likeness, and He provides all we need and more. He made the heavens and the Earth. He holds the universe in His hands. He raised us from the dust of the Earth and stitched us together in our mother's womb. He laid down His life for us on a Friday and conquered death for us on Sunday. He is coming soon.

Spiritual Weapons for Spiritual Battle

For we do not wrestle against flesh and
blood, but against the rulers, against the
authorities, against the cosmic powers over

> *this present darkness, against the spiri-*
> *tual forces of evil in the heavenly places.*
> —Ephesians 6:12, ESV

Many Christians seem to have forgotten that the battles we fight are not really political, but spiritual. Many Christians, particularly in America, have been looking for political saviors to help them withstand the forces of the world. But those political saviors cannot protect or save us, and Christians would do well to remember that. Instead of giving in to fear or getting angry, we should fight spiritual battles with spiritual weapons. As Paul reminds us:

> Therefore take up the whole armor of God, that you may be able to withstand in the evil day, and having done all, to stand firm. Stand therefore, having fastened on the belt of truth, and having put on the breastplate of righteousness, and, as shoes for your feet, having put on the readiness given by the gospel of peace. In all circumstances take up the shield of faith, with which you can extinguish all the flaming darts of the evil one; and take the helmet of salvation, and the sword of the Spirit, which is the word of God, praying at all times in the Spirit, with all prayer and sup-plication. (Ephesians 6:13–18, ESV)

We are dealing with spiritual warfare. The secular world does not understand and cannot grapple with it. The fight we have right now is a fight the church is best equipped to lead. But have you noticed what is happening to churches?

The church itself is bogged down in secular fights. Congregations are squabbling internally over political fights. In some congregations, fidelity to Donald Trump is more important than faithfulness to Jesus Christ. This is because some in the church presume that fidelity to Trump automatically means one is faithful to Jesus. However, actual faithfulness to Jesus can lead to being rejected by some Christians. Pastors who address the need for racial reconciliation are labeled liberal.

Satan is running through churches. The spiritual fight is here. For those of you in the church, your commitment to the truth of Christ is more important than ever. You cannot hide from the world. You must engage the world—the Great Commission demands it.

But how you engage the world matters. You must engage with love, and you must love your neighbor—even the Democrats, the gay, the transgendered, the woke, and the skeptic. You must seek the welfare of your community and pray for it. You will find your welfare there.

Stop fretting about Washington so much unless you live there. Washington has no answers for the spiritual problems we face. You do, and, at your local level, you can address them through prayer, community engagement, and the church.

The church must rise. Satan is keeping us divided. Take each other's word. Give each room to disagree on matters not essential to salvation. Preach and teach the gospel. Engage your community. The fight we are in is a fight for souls. So, stop treating it as a political fight.

King David wrote in Psalm 27:3: "Though an army encamp against me, my heart shall not fear; though war arise against me, yet

I will be confident." We should be more like David and trust in the Lord. Remember God's promises to His people: "I have chosen you and not cast you off; fear not, for I am with you; be not dismayed, for I am your God; I will strengthen you, I will help you, I will uphold you with my righteous right hand." (Isaiah 41:9–10, ESV)

Hope in Times of Fear

> *The Lord is my helper; I will not*
> *fear; what can man do to me?*
> —Hebrews 13:6, ESV

Well-known author and pastor Timothy Keller was diagnosed with stage IV pancreatic cancer in 2020. Like most people who receive a terminal diagnosis, Keller went through the full range of emotions, including fear, grief, anxiety, disbelief, and ultimately acceptance. While we all know that we will die eventually, being faced with your mortality changes your priorities for the time you have left. As Keller said: "[Knowing] you are really are going to die changes the way you look at your time, the way you look at God, the way you look at your spouse. Everything just changes when you actually realize time is limited and I'm mortal."[148]

Keller continued to read the Scriptures, pray, teach, and write as he went through chemotherapy. He was particularly encouraged by the promise and reality of the Resurrection. He published his reflections on the Resurrection in *Hope in Times of Fear: The*

---

[148] Leah MarieAnn Klett, "Tim Keller Shares Cancer Update, Says Facing Mortality Has Transformed His Prayer Life," *The Christian Post*, January 7, 2023, https://www.christianpost.com/news/tim-keller-shares-cancer-update-prayer-life-transformation.html.

Resurrection and the Meaning of Easter. I had the opportunity to talk with him about the book on my radio show.[149]

We discussed how at the beginning of his book, Keller writes about the word *hope*. We tend to use the word hope as a wish. I hope I get a promotion. I hope my kid does well in school. That is not what the Greek word *elpida*, translated as *hope*, means in Scripture.

When Paul writes about hope in Romans or the author of Hebrews writes about hope, they are writing about confidence. Our hope in the Resurrection is our confidence or profound certainty in the Resurrection. Our faith gives us courage because we are confident in and certain of our future in Christ.

As Christians, we talk often about Jesus's life and death, what His sacrifice means for us, and how we should live as Christians. These are all important topics, but we tend to move too quickly past the empty tomb when we should spend a lot of time meditating on the Resurrection. The Resurrection is the one event in human history that has the power to change you, unlike Caesar crossing the Rubicon or Washington crossing the Delaware.

The Resurrection is the central event that defines Christianity. That's why when Paul was arrested and brought before the Jewish leaders, he said, "It is with respect to the hope and the resurrection of the dead that I am on trial." (Acts 23:6, ESV) Without Jesus's Resurrection, we have no hope in this life or the next. As Paul wrote:

> If Christ has not been raised, then our preaching is in vain and your faith is in vain.... For if

[149] Erick Erickson, "Hope in Times of Fear: An Interview with Rev. Tim Keller," The Erick Erickson Show, April 2, 2021, https://ewerickson.substack.com/p/hope-in-times-of-fear.

the dead are not raised, not even Christ has been
raised. And if Christ has not been raised, your
faith is futile and you are still in your sins. Then
those also who have fallen asleep in Christ have
perished. If in Christ we have hope in this life
only, we are of all people most to be pitied. (1
Corinthians 15:14,16–19, ESV)

Our hope in the Resurrection is what sets us apart as believers. It's how we can face everything from terminal cancer diagnoses to persecution. Atheists often ask me how I can believe in a God who would let my wife go through cancer. And I try, as graciously as I can, to point to our hope in the Resurrection. Jesus died and was raised for us. Because my wife is a believer, I know she'll have eternal life. When our loved ones die, we grieve, and that's appropriate. The Scriptures tell us, though, that we do not grieve like the world does, without hope:

For since we believe that Jesus died and rose
again, even so, through Jesus, God will bring
with him those who have fallen asleep.… For the
Lord himself will descend from heaven with a
cry of command, with the voice of an archangel,
and with the sound of the trumpet of God. And
the dead in Christ will rise first. Then we who
are alive, who are left, will be caught up together
with them in the clouds to meet the Lord in
the air, and so we will always be with the Lord.
Therefore encourage one another with these
words. (1 Thessalonians 4:14, 16–18, ESV)

Keller explained another point he likes to make when people ask him why God would allow him to suffer. He tells people who ask, that, even though we don't understand the reasons why we suffer, we do know there is meaning and purpose in our suffering. If you don't believe in God, then your suffering is meaningless. It's just part of the way the world works: The strong eat the weak, only the fit survive, nature is red in tooth and claw. Suffering has no meaning.

But if there is a God and He has actually come into the world and suffered with us, we know that He cares about us and our suffering. Through His Resurrection, Jesus showed us that God will do something about our suffering in the end.

When people say, "Why did Tim get cancer?" His answer is that there's at least 200 million reasons, good reasons that we have no idea about. But he knows that even though he may never know exactly why he has cancer, he knows that it isn't because God doesn't love him and his family. Keller knows Jesus lived, died, and then rose again to give us an absolute confidence that when we die, we'll be with God forever. We can trust in God because He is in control, and He is with us.

Trust in God

> *Fear not, for I am with you; be not dis-*
> *mayed, for I am your God; I will strengthen*
> *you, I will help you, I will uphold you*
> *with my righteous right hand.*
> —Isaiah 41:10, ESV

Are you familiar with the story of God making the covenant with Abraham? In Genesis 1, the God of all Creation told Abraham that his descendants, God's chosen people, were going to be enslaved for 400 years. Before it even happened, God had planned it and had His reasons for it.

He let the Israelites suffer in Egypt until the iniquity of the Amorites was complete. In so doing, He was balancing His justice. The Amorites were a pagan, idolatrous people, but they had not piled up their sins so much for God to punish them. He let them have their way for 400 years and then used the Israelites as His instrument of judgment against them.

Remember, in general, the wicked have what appears to be a better life than God's people because God is letting them have their fill of the world as a bit of mercy. This life really will be the best they ever have. Notice, too, that God rules over and punishes the wicked, even though they don't recognize Him as their God.

At times, God allows His own people to suffer for a while, but He then delivers them into great blessings, as He did with His people in Egypt. In fact, God let the Amorites build up cities and wealth to hand it over to His people, as He did with the Egyptians. God takes care of and provides for His children.

We may be in a season of wondering what God is doing and why He doesn't seem to be answering our prayers or telling us why He is making us wait. Maybe our political leaders aren't the ones we wanted. Inflation may be high, and the economy may be weak. We may be out of work and wondering how we will feed our families. As Christians, we may be experiencing increasing persecution.

Forget all that for a moment. Please. Forget that. Some of it makes you excited. Some of it gives you anxiety. Put those things aside and remember this. God Himself came to Earth in the lowliest state. Born in a manger and raised by a carpenter and his wife,

Christ came to restore our relationship with the Father, undone in the fall.

Just think about that for a moment.

All of human history, we waited for what God promised in the garden—that a descendant of Eve would have a son who would crush the head of the serpent. Adam and Eve hoped it would be Seth, whose name means "appointed." But it was not him. Noah's family hoped it would be Noah, whose name means "rest" like the Sabbath rest at last.

For generations, humanity waited, and then, of all places, Jesus, God with us, was born in a stable and placed in a manger. Now, we here wait again for Him to return, as generations of Christians have before us. We do not know when. But Jesus will return in all His glory and call us to Him.

In the meantime, in the anxiety and anxiousness of the present fallen world, we can stay informed. We can stay engaged. But we have to remember something vital.

We need no king, no political savior, and no political party to win. We have already won because Christ is King, He has won, and He will return.

We've won. Let not your heart be troubled. Do not be anxious. Regardless of electoral outcomes, political leaders, wars, rumors of wars, and the troubles of this planet, victory is already ours. It is, as they say, darkest before the dawn. The troubles of the world seem to be spiraling out of control. Darkness seems even darker than before.

But God draws near, and the light is coming again. So do not fear. Do not be anxious. God is sovereign. He has a plan. While we in our temporal schemes voted for or against the incoming president, God—infinite, eternal, and, above all, determining the outcome in His sovereign will—still points to Christ.

Those of you who are nervous, fretful, and fearful of what the future holds need to rely on Scripture. Do not worry about tomorrow. We may not always understand these things and we may sometimes think it looks like evil is prevailing, but God is not mocked, and He cannot be defeated. God is good all the time, and He will prevail. We can trust in God.

Through the events going on today, God is smashing idols. Christians who are angry or fretful need to understand that ultimately this pulls us closer to Christ. Christ has conquered, and character does matter. Your job is to glorify God in all you do as you seek the welfare of the community in which you live and pray for it.

Christians should behave prudently. Christians should not live in fear. Distinguishing between the two can be difficult. When we are tempted to respond in fear, we need to take a step back and remember that God is still on His throne. He is still sovereign.

The God of the universe who created all things, sent bread from heaven, provided water from rocks, and raised Christ from the dead is still in control. We know that all things work for the good of those called according to His purposes, and we can see glimpses of good even now.

As we saw during the pandemic, people are reaching out to care for others, especially the vulnerable and elderly, in our communities. We see a recognition again that life is precious. Jesus has one task—to build His church. There is no plan B. The gates of hell will not prevail against that mission.

Even when our physical church buildings were closed, and even if they are closed in the future, the spiritual church, the body of Christ, can still open hearts to prayer, wallets to charity, and themselves to serving others. The church can show the world that Jesus's mission continues no matter what happens around us.

Fear not, because God is with us. Fear not, because God is on His throne. Fear not, because the God of all Creation is working everything for His purposes, even when we cannot see or understand. We can understand He's got a plan for us. The plan is on His timetable, not ours. Sometimes we have to keep waiting until God is ready to deliver to us to the land of milk and honey.

Patience and perseverance can be hard but are less hard when you understand God is working even if we don't see it. The story of the Resurrection is a story that began before time. Your story began and will continue in eternity. This life is temporary and even here, in the temporary, you can't see the next chapter, but it is coming. So, too, is the King. God will help us and uphold us even when all else fails. So, trust in God.

Keep Your Eyes Fixed on Jesus

> *Therefore, since we are surrounded by so great*
> *a cloud of witnesses, let us also lay aside every*
> *weight, and sin which clings so closely, and let*
> *us run with endurance the race that is set before*
> *us, looking to Jesus, the founder and perfecter*
> *of our faith, who for the joy that was set before*
> *him endured the cross, despising the shame, and*
> *is seated at the right hand of the throne of God.*
> —Hebrews 12:1–2, ESV

When the king of Syria sent an army to capture the prophet Elisha, Elisha's servant saw the soldiers and horses and cried out in fear. Elisha comforted his servant and prayed that he would be able to see what was really going on. The servant was amazed when his eyes were opened. He finally saw the reality of their situation. God had surrounded them with an army of angels who stood ready to protect them.

Elisha then dealt with the Syrian army. He prayed for God to blind them and then led them far away. Instead of letting the king of Israel destroy the Syrians, Elisha prayed for their eyes to be healed and told the king to give the soldiers food and water and send them back home. (2 Kings 6) Elisha's mercy and grace toward the men sent to harm him is hard for us to understand.

The blind see the light and realize where they are. They realize God is with Elisha and leave. The response is not to slaughter them, but to treat them kindly—to satisfy their actual hunger. Elisha was the one whom others sought, looked up to, listened to, and respected because he knew to rely on God, not panic, and treated others—even those who would capture or kill him—with grace and mercy. He showed patience with his servant who could not see despite having seen miracles. He showed gentleness to the king. He showed firmness and charity to an enemy.

There are a lot of people right now who cannot bring themselves to treat their opponents with mercy and kindness. More and more people see the other side as their enemy. Political differences are now attacks. Competing philosophies are now treason. It makes sense for the godless. Politics is, for many of them, their religion.

But for the Christian, things should be different. We have an obligation to truth, and we have an angel army with us. Too many people of faith are blinded by their anger right now. They don't see the angel army. They forget God is sovereign and in charge. They are more wrapped up in the America of their mind than the God of their reality. They need prayer. We all need prayer. How often are you praying for yourself and others to see God's presence in our lives?

We head into even more trying times as a nation moving forward. We need to pray for ourselves and others that God opens our and their eyes to His presence and pray for encouragement. We need to be more charitable to others and break bread with those with whom we disagree.

There's an army of angels around us who surround us and protect us. They battle for us. This season of our lives will pass. Whether we're closer to God or the world after it passes will depend on how we live today.

In Romans 8:18, Paul wrote, "For I consider that the sufferings of this present time are not worth comparing with the glory that is to be revealed to us." (ESV) That "glory that is to be revealed" is the future that awaits us with Christ. We are headed toward a great reveal. The things unseen will be seen. Every day moves us closer to that revelation. We do not know the day, but we get closer each day, and all of Creation groans for it. As part of Creation—creatures created in the image of God, we groan for it most of all.

When people in the streets protest, they likely aren't aware, but their groans and cries for justice are part of Creation's groaning. When we first become aware as children, we begin to question things. We hear that voice that comes from our soul asking why we are here, what our purpose is, whether there is something better, and why this world is so unjust and unfair.

The world tells us that there is no purpose, when we die the worms eat us, and the secret to happiness is to enjoy what we can while we can. The world co-opts true religion and twists it, just as sin has twisted everything. We expect and want justice because the world was created by a just God. The world twists our desire for justice into power struggles and striving for man-created justice.

As discussed, when people reject Christianity, religion does not just go away. Secularism takes on sacraments, liturgy, rite, and ritual. We are witnessing, in real time in the streets, the new Gnosticism settling on its orthodoxies and creeds. Abortion is a sacrament. "Black lives matter" is a liturgy and creed that must be strictly adhered to. Protest replaces worship services. Riots are revival.

Creation groans for justice and righteousness, and those created in God's image groan the loudest and bear the greatest burdens. Those who have hope put their trust in the Creator Who they know will return. Those who have given in to the voices of the world and abandoned the Creator have abandoned hope. They put their trust in the people around them, who are sinners just like them. They have no hope of anything better and are intent on delivering heaven on Earth. But internally, the groaning they feel is longing for *real* heaven on Earth.

Christians need to tell others the truth of our hope in Christ. The souls of those marching in the street groan because all the world can feel the return of the King approaching. We do not know when. But we inwardly feel it.

Christians need to be preaching Jesus, not merely Christian values or politics. We need to preach about the Resurrection and return and the world made new. It is fantastical and supernatural and unbelievable for so many. But it is real and right and true and is the only hope for the hopeless. The world groans and cries out for justice. No protest or riot will give true justice. But there is something better coming—there is some*one* better coming. He will make all things new, deliver justice, and wipe away tears.

This week, you will encounter ideas, people, positions, and more that you don't like. You'll find causes you care about or deeply oppose. Don't care about them or oppose them so much that you make an idol of them. More than any impact Washington will ever have, you have the ability to have a greater impact by reflecting Christ and glorifying God in both what you do and how you do it.

In the grand scheme of all eternity, the concerns of the present world matter far less than Christ's empty tomb. The truth is, Christ is more important than anything in American politics, and no American politician or mob can stop the advance of the Kingdom of God. So today, focus on eternity, not Washington. Take some time to reset your outlook. The King is coming.

> *Then I saw a new heaven and a new earth, for the first heaven and the first earth had passed away, and the sea was no more. And I saw the holy city, new Jerusalem, coming down out of heaven from God, prepared as a bride adorned for her husband. And I heard a loud voice from the throne saying, "Behold, the dwelling place of*

God is with man. He will dwell with them, and they will be his people, and God himself will be with them as their God. He will wipe away every tear from their eyes, and death shall be no more, neither shall there be mourning, nor crying, nor pain anymore, for the former things have passed away." And he who was seated on the throne said, "Behold, I am making all things new."
—Revelation 21:1–5, ESV

ACKNOWLEDGMENTS

Special thanks to Bill Blankschaen whose friendship and guidance helped me put words to page and pushed me to keep going deeper.